BELIEVE
TRAINING JOURNAL

BY PRO RUNNERS
LAUREN FLESHMAN &
RÓISÍN MCGETTIGAN–DUMAS

VELO press

Boulder, Colorado

▼velopress®

3002 Sterling Circle, Suite 100
Boulder, Colorado 80301-2338 USA
(303) 440-0601 / Fax (303) 444-6788 / E-mail velopress@competitorgroup.com

Distributed in the United States and Canada by Ingram Publisher Services

Library of Congress Control Number: 2014945152
ISBN: 978-1-937715-28-1

For information on purchasing VeloPress books,
please call (800) 811-4210, ext. 2138, or visit www.velopress.com.

Cover design by Anna Kalbrener
Interior design by Vicki Hopewell
Photo retouching by Elizabeth Riley
Illustration on p. 121 by Sally Bergesen
Photos courtesy of Lauren Fleshman: pp. 11, 39, 55, 89, 135, 151, 165, 181, 195, 227
Additional photos: p. 1 (photo of Lauren Fleshman) and p. 117, Mark Stone/Stone Photography;
    p. 1 (photo of Róisín McGettigan-Dumas), Jen Brister; p. 17, Mark Dadswell/Getty Images;
    pp. 75 and 105, Myles Dumas; p. 211, AP Photo/Sang Tan

14 15 16 / 10 9 8 7 6 5 4 3

CONTENTS

Goal Setting 18
Dream big and define your goals for the coming year

Approach 40
Know yourself and your blind spots before you get started

Physical Training & Workouts 56
Be intentional with your method, work in plenty of variety,
and have fun

Mental Training 76
Understand how your mind affects performance and work
it to your advantage

Nutrition 90
Establish good eating habits to boost performance

Body Image 106
Learn how to love what you've got

Lauren Fleshman has been a runner since she was 13 years old and 78 pounds of scrawny, scrappy tomboy. She is a five-time NCAA champion and two-time USA champion. Her plan is to compete professionally through the 2016 Olympics, try to set PRs from 800 meters up to the marathon, and have a hell of a good time doing it and writing about it. Find her blog at asklaurenfleshman.com and look for her column, "The Fast Life," in *Runner's World* magazine. Lauren is married to professional triathlete Jesse Thomas, and they are the proud parents of Jude. They live and train in Bend, Oregon, where their energy bar company, Picky Bars, is based.

Róisín McGettigan-Dumas grew up running the beaches, trails, and roads of Wicklow, Ireland. She left home for a chance to compete in track and cross-country at Providence College, where she was a four-time All-American. In 2008 Ro represented Ireland in the 3K steeplechase at the Olympics. She was awarded the bronze medal in the 1500 meters at the 2009 European Indoor Championships and still holds the Irish record for the indoor mile. While she's retired from running competitively, Ro remains invested in the sport as an entrepreneur and certified sports psychology consultant in Providence, Rhode Island, where she lives, trains, and juggles family life with her husband, Myles, and daughters, Hope and Ava.

INTRODUCTION

As pro runners, we've been fortunate to travel and race all over the world. We set out to create the ideal journal for ourselves and for other female athletes based on the things we've learned along the way. We run distances from 800 meters to the marathon, and we have competed from the youth ranks all the way to the Olympics.

Over the years, we've raced for fun, for national pride, for money, and for charity, and no matter the distance or the reason, our best races and experiences happen when our mind and body are working together and we are making the time every day to give ourselves credit for our efforts.

Believe Training Journal is designed to guide your running to the best place possible. It is one part training log, one part how-to manual, and one part workbook—all woven into one year of your life. The purpose is to get you to the sweet spot for performance, where heart meets intellect and effort meets ease. To get you to a place of knowledge and balance. To help you set, stick to, and accomplish your goals, and use running as a tool to enhance your overall life.

Throughout these pages, you'll find motivation from us, from leading research, and from sisters in sport all over the world; but most of all, as you fill out this journal, you'll find inspiration in your personal journey.

Your Training Log

There's no prescription for training and racing that works for everyone. By taking action and then reflecting on the whole process, you will cultivate awareness and discover what works and what doesn't. This information can empower your decision making and give you confidence in your preparation.

Start using the journal anytime—the pages are undated. Use the annual calendar to write down any races or lay out important training blocks in the months ahead. And since running happens in the context of everything else going on in life, you can use this space for personal events such as birthdays, weddings, and vacations, too.

To make good use of the weekly training log, you'll need to develop a system for entering your details that allows you to see the data and patterns at a glance. We've deliberately kept the layout simple so you can easily track the basics—how far, how fast, how it felt—yet have some room left over for other things that are important to you. For suggestions of how to handle this, check out the excerpts from our own training journals and our list of things to track:

workout ✳ distance ✳ pace ✳ how it felt ✳ conditions ✳ terrain ✳ drills ✳ rest days ✳ races ✳ events ✳ injuries ✳ gratitude ✳ gym sessions ✳ yoga/stretching ✳ PT/massage ✳ iron levels ✳ mood ✳ weight ✳ social events ✳ sleep ✳ travel ✳ new shoes ✳ period ✳ things of note ✳ heart rate

There are also free writing spaces interspersed throughout the journal. Use these pages for notes, goal updates, race reviews, and extra writing/doodling/dreaming/to-do space.

"I record things that help me see my growth both physically and mentally, and see how I pushed through things I didn't think I could. My journal is a piece of me and who I am."
DOTTIE LESSARD, U.S. TRANSPLANT GAMES GOLD MEDALIST, COACH & AUTHOR

"Filling in my log is part of my nightly routine. It doesn't take long to do, yet it's great for tracking training data and body cycles. With this info I can predict my best weeks for optimal training and racing." STEPHANIE REILLY, OLYMPIAN

"My log makes me remember the friends and the fun on each of the runs—from mile repeats in the pouring rain to the glorious Sunday long runs."
MARY WITTENBERG, NEW YORK ROAD RUNNERS PRESIDENT & CEO

"I started recording hours of sleep later in college because I kept getting phantom viruses and the only cure is proper rest."
ANN GAFFIGAN, USA CHAMPION & COFOUNDER OF WOMEN TALK SPORTS

"If I feel uninspired to get out the door, I'm motivated by the fact that I have to record something in that day's box; otherwise it will remain forever blank."
MALINDI ELMORE, OLYMPIAN

Obstacles you might face:

Distraction, loss of energy
from being a mom, inadequate
sleep, too much travel

DATE	WORKOUT		MILEAGE / RATING
MON 10/13	Day off Yeah Baby!	(massage)	0 ++
TUES 10/14	Hill repeats @ Meadow camp (1x3', 3x1')x3 w/ walk down Rec. Felt strong til last set. Knee a tiny bit sore but better than Sunday!	(Gym)	9 +
WED 10/15	am 4mi. easy (ugh) pm 8mi. easy Shevlin Park gorgeous and relaxed	(core)	12 -/+
THURS 10/16 (★)	6mi. tempo 2mi. @ 6:00 2m @ 5:50 2m @ 5:35 HR controlled Last 5 min. tough but I was mentally strong		10 ++

"Dwell in positivity. It's worth the effort."
LAUREN FLESHMAN

DATE	WORKOUT		MILEAGE / RATING
FRI 10/17	am 6 mi. w/ Mel + Christine @ Deschutes Trail	(Core)	6
	pm 45 min. swim, tired/unmotivated		+/−
SAT 10/18 ⭐	8 x 400 at Track w/ 90"R 74, 74, 73, 74, 72, 72, 73, 70 followed by 60' Run Smooth, felt looonng. <u>Good</u>	(GYM)	11 ++
SUN 10/19 ↑ Mom's BDay!	Long Run 13m Green Lake, last time before the snow closure! <u>SO AWESOME</u>		13 +

| | TOTAL | 61 |

{ RUNDOWN } Great week overall. Knee cleared up 95% and hit the workouts well. Skipped core a couple days ☹ but great progress. Was on <u>time</u>! Can I keep this up?!

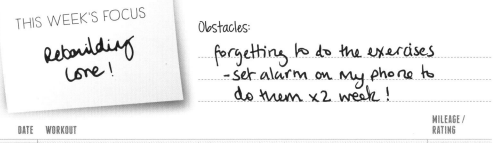

THIS WEEK'S FOCUS

Rebuilding
core !

Obstacles:

forgetting to do the exercises
- set alarm on my phone to
do them x2 week !

DATE	WORKOUT	MILEAGE / RATING
MON 6/30	6mi. pool w/ steph + kids ☺	6 ☺
TUES 7/1	6mi. 🍷 world cup ran in pm. still buzzing	6 ☺
WED 7/2	Run w/ Ro grp HOT: pm 2mi. + 10 x min. + core + 2mi. picnic in park	5 ☺
THURS 7/3	am PT - getting stronger 3.5 mi. to Molly's — fun Humid but enjoyable	3.5 ☺

"Your worst enemy cannot harm you as much as your own thoughts, unguarded. But once mastered, no one can help you as much." BUDDHA

DATE	WORKOUT	MILEAGE / RATING
FRI 7/4	5 mi. in Rain ☺	5
	Emen's - tired zzz	
	* Baby is 12 weeks old ☺	
SAT 7/5	3 steady - no time	3
	CT all day - nice	
SUN 7/6	4 mi. - tired - PT exercises zzz	4
	garden stuff	
	work stuff	☺
		TOTAL

{ RUNDOWN } Busy with lots going on this week. Need to schedule in some yoga !! Keep up PT exercises

7

Your How-to Manual

A balanced approach to sport optimizes performance while minimizing the chance of experiencing unnecessary setbacks. Think of sport as a wheel. The day you caught the desire to be an athlete, you were handed a floppy tire tube. To go far and fast you need to build a functioning, strong wheel. With our journal we hope to make the process of becoming a well-rounded athlete simple and fun.

The center of the wheel, the hub, is built when you start to visualize your athletic potential and make competitive goals. It's the focal point that everything rotates around. But the strength of the wheel is its supporting structure. Those spokes connect your desire and passion and time spent training to your goals and your ambition.

+ Physical training
+ Mental training
+ Nutrition
+ Recovery techniques
+ Life balance
+ Competition
+ Community

Your wheel may have more spokes than this, but it should not have fewer. If you build those spokes *evenly* over time, your wheel will be strong and will carry you with relative ease through your athletic endeavors. With this approach in mind, we've devoted each month of this journal to a subject that plays a critical role in performance. Our intention is to help you navigate the overload of information and focus on what we've personally found to be most helpful.

You can read ahead or tackle the 12 topics over the course of your season, but keep in mind that all of the spokes are equally important. Put too much emphasis on one spoke or ignore another, and your wheel becomes weak and collapses beneath you. For example, on the topic of nutrition, many runners get stuck: *Looking* the part of a distance runner becomes more important than actually running fast! Think about how lopsided and wonky your wheel will roll with one overbuilt spoke.

Everyone gets out of whack at some point. There's no shame in screwing up. It's a necessary part of reaching out into the unknown of your potential. The only shame would be in not using the resources at your disposal to get yourself back in balance. Use the table of contents to pick out topics that you know you need to address early in your season.

Your Workbook

Over the course of the year, we'll share what we think you need to know, but it's up to you to work out what each topic means for you and your training. You'll find worksheets, quizzes, lists, exercises, and plenty of space for notes. Our hope is that you bring this mindfulness into your entire month and experiment with it in your daily life. To help you stay on track, we've added plenty of prompts and quotes to serve as motivation, inspiration, or a kick in the butt!

We believe that this little journal will make you a better athlete. But don't just take our word for it. Our friends, mentors, and sisters in sport agree that keeping a training journal is time well spent. Plus, science says so! When we write things down (the retro way, with pen and paper), it actually helps us develop motor memory and spurs motivation to exercise again. Take a couple of minutes after your workout to record the day's effort and boost your running. And your journal will be even more powerful if you don't limit it to running. Never underestimate the impact of other life events on performance. Include notes about major things happening outside your

training—family stress, social events, work deadlines, etc.

So now what? Set some goals, chart your course, and start recording the things that are important to you. There may be a detour or two along the way, but as you develop your skills you'll be able to handle them like a pro. After a year with this journal, we are confident you'll be a stronger, more knowledge-able, and more satisfied runner, anchored by the ability to aim high and BELIEVE.

Your sisters in sport,

Lauren & Ro

Dos and Don'ts for Beginners

If you're just getting started on your running journey, a little extra know-how will make your experience more fun and rewarding.

Do get a decent pair of running shoes.

Don't try to increase the distance and speed of your run at the same time.

Do mix up the paces of your runs. You'll find some of our favorite workouts on pp. 58–63.

Don't jump up in weekly mileage quickly. Build slowly.

Don't run hard two days in a row. Aim for 2–3 hard days (workouts/tempo/long run/race) in a week max.

Do set some goals. Then find a coach, or find a training plan to work from.

Do establish consistency in your training. No matter what level you are aiming to get to, finding consistency is very helpful.

Don't forget to write down what you've done. It increases the likelihood of doing it again.

Do some glute exercises— they make you a more resilient runner.

Do add in running drills to enhance your form and efficiency.

Do eat a snack within 30 minutes of training to boost your metabolism and to aid recovery.

Don't worry about how fast you are going. Just focus on not stopping.

Do run more—it gets easier. But keep in mind that it's always going to be a little hard. Embrace the effort and discomfort. Your brain and your body like it.

Finally, **do** find a flock! Having some training partners helps keep you accountable, makes you less likely to skip workouts, and makes runs more fun. Even meeting someone one day a week will break up the week for you. Local running stores usually have the lowdown about running groups in your area. Clubs and group runs are a great place to befriend people of all ages and walks of life.

BELIEVE IN YOUR MINDFULNESS

ANNUAL CALENDAR

MONTH	01	02	03	04	05	06	07	08	09	10	11	12	13	14	15

16	17	18	19	20	21	22	23	24	25	26	27	28	29	30	31

ANNUAL CALENDAR

MONTH	01	02	03	04	05	06	07	08	09	10	11	12	13	14	15

16	17	18	19	20	21	22	23	24	25	26	27	28	29	30	31

HUMBLE
realistic
RESILIENT OPEN
BE CONSISTENT commit
SELF-AWARE ACCEPT FAILURE DO THE
FOCUS WORK

BELIEVE IN YOUR GOALS

DEFINING YOUR GOALS

Sometimes what you want is glaringly obvious. You are determined to run the Boston Marathon and you know exactly what splits you need to run in order to get that qualifier. Other times you might feel more ambivalent about what you want. The desire is still there, but it might be time to turn up the volume. Identifying what you truly want is the first step toward a more inspired way of living.

My Olympic dream began when I was a child, and it guided my life for almost 20 years. However, it was the yearly, monthly, weekly, and daily goal-setting that really navigated my route to the Olympics. It was truly an adventure, and along the way I learned some hard lessons about actualizing my dreams. I've coupled my insights with the latest psychology research to help you set, stick to, and accomplish your goals.

Dare to Dream

There are two sides of the brain competing for attention: the rational mind and the creative mind. Both are useful, but the rational mind often takes over, limiting your horizon. When imagining the future, you must allow the powerful creative intelligence of your feelings and intuition to guide you. An architect doesn't begin building a skyscraper by thinking about square footage, electrical wiring, and a complete list of materials; she starts by envisioning what the finished product will look like, how it will feel inside, and how it will be used. Once she has a clear vision of the final product, she then makes a plan to build it. Give yourself the freedom to dream without regard for what is or isn't possible—there will be time later to sort out the details.

Close the Gap

The space between where you now stand and where you want to be can create a great force of energy. When you are excited about the possibilities that await you, it results in enthusiasm, motivation, and drive. This is why setting goals is so useful. Are you looking for increased motivation to train? Sign up for some races that excite you, or set some goal times that inspire you. Keep aiming to close the gap. Keep improving. Keep changing. Keep growing. And if you arrive at your goal, aim higher, farther, faster. You'll reach beyond what you ever thought possible.

Fuel Persistence with Purpose

Meaningful goals act as a catalyst, increasing energy, improving decision making, and strengthening commitment. Most adventures will include detours or setbacks, so if you're not truly enthusiastic about your goals, it's easy to become dejected, lack fortitude, and give up. Your sense of *purpose* is what keeps you on track. It gives you the persistence to grind, stretch, fall down, stand up, overcome, improve habits, and make better choices.

The Journey Is the Reward

The media would have us believe that the outcome determines success. However, the leading sports psychologists, authors, and spiritual gurus agree that it's more beneficial to focus on the process than on the outcome. When you embrace each step along the way, regardless of the final outcome, *you win*. While I did make it to the Olympics, in my heart and soul I feel my true success was having lived the athlete's life. I was able to be a fully committed athlete in the sport I loved, and the lifestyle of traveling, training, and racing will stay with me forever, as will the friends. **RMD**

Supercharge Your Chance of Success

☀ Set process goals, not outcome goals

This keeps your goals in a realm where you can dictate the commitment you make and the effort you put in. Goals focused on a particular outcome will potentially put you up against other athletes, weather conditions, or other details that are out of your hands.

☀ You can have it all, but not at the same time!

Decide what goals are most important to you. Choose which goals you will focus on and when. Leaning in one direction means pulling away from something else, even for a little while. Saying yes to your goals could also mean saying no to other plans. Drop the shoulds and the guilt.

☀ Embrace the power of negative thoughts

Research shows that people who anticipate obstacles and pro-actively think of ways around them are more likely to achieve a goal than those who skip this step. Better to look ahead and prepare than to look back and regret.

☀ Keep goals visible

Anything that keeps your goal at the forefront of your mind will help it remain a priority. Believe in yourself. Studies show that successful people have a vision and go for it!

☀ Watch your words

Declare what you want, not what you don't want. "I want to feel fit and fast" is better than "I don't want to be fat and out of shape."

☀ Share your goals

Tell someone—your coach, sister in sport, spouse—anyone who will help keep you accountable!

☀ Reward yourself

You might think this is frivolous, that the intrinsic reward by itself is enough, but your emotional brain wants you to feel good. A reward (or punish-ment, as preferred by some people) will keep you motivated to continuously raise your game.

☀ Make the time

Carve out time in your day to work on your goal. By scheduling it, you'll be less likely to forget about it.

Dare to DREAM

Use these questions and prompts to brainstorm what goals you want to set and what you need to do to reach them. Give yourself space to do this. Go for a run and listen to your thoughts. Contemplate what you really want. Be present and see what arises for you.

What would you attempt to do if you knew you could not fail? What How would you like to FEEL in the coming year—fit, energized,

I want to be able to run 4x
per week. I want to push myself
to keep going even when I feel
like I might fall over & die I
want to be able to jog 1 mile
in 10 min max & run 1 mile
with out stopping. I want to be
less lazy & create less excuses. I
may even try getting up
before work and fitting in a quick
1/2 - full mile. Going to work
energized, come home, cook,
clean, eat, & run 1 mile again
shower & relax :)

4/8/15

(right margin, rotated) do you want to achieve in terms of performance? Where do your

(left margin, rotated) stands in the way of your goals? What does your ideal day look like?

(right margin, rotated) successful, connected, inspired, alive?

(bottom margin, rotated) aspirations come from—past performances, training, dreams? What

GOALS *Lauren*

Qualify for World Champs in the 5k

- I love traveling + competing with the best in the world!
- I want to have a chance to fight for a medal
- I want to represent my country + the companies and people who have supported me for years!
- There's more fast in these legs!

- Smart training plan from coach w/my input
- Racing schedule that sets me up to qualify
- Race under 15:25 for 5k
- Finish top 3 at USA Champs in June
- Race XC to get strong in the winter
- Circuits + Gym in the fall
- Consistent mileage 60-75 mi./week + body work

GOALS

1. Use this space to set goals in more than one area of your life, for example, mind (education, work), body (sport, health), soul (social, family life).

2. Define the *intentions* or reasons behind each goal. This will sustain your energy and commitment.

3. Identify the steps you'll need to take to achieve each goal.

GOAL

feel fit & energetic
on sport & life
Racing 5k's

REASONS

+ energy for the kids
+ energy for work
+ love competing + getting after it
+ get in shape post-baby

STEPS

+ get to bed by 1030! Up + Run in am.
+ meet girls x1/week
+ push myself x1-2/week
+ find + attend yoga x1/week
+ keep up PT exercises
+ use BWD 5k's to test myself.

Make your GOALS take shape

GOAL

REASONS

STEPS

"Setting goals gives your life meaning. The feeling of setting a goal, working hard, and then achieving it is the best."   SARAH JAMIESON, OLYMPIAN & COMMONWEALTH GAMES SILVER MEDALIST

GOAL

REASONS

STEPS

GOALS

GOAL

REASONS

STEPS

"If you can dream it, with intention, you can do it."
DEEPAK CHOPRA, AUTHOR, PHYSICIAN & LECTURER

GOAL

REASONS

STEPS

THIS WEEK'S FOCUS

Things you're excited about:

....

....

....

DATE	WORKOUT	MILEAGE / RATING
MON		
TUES		
WED		
THURS		

*"If you want to become the best runner you can be, start now.
Don't spend the rest of your life wondering if you can do it."*
PRISCILLA WELCH, BRITISH ARMY OFFICER TURNED OLYMPIC MARATHONER

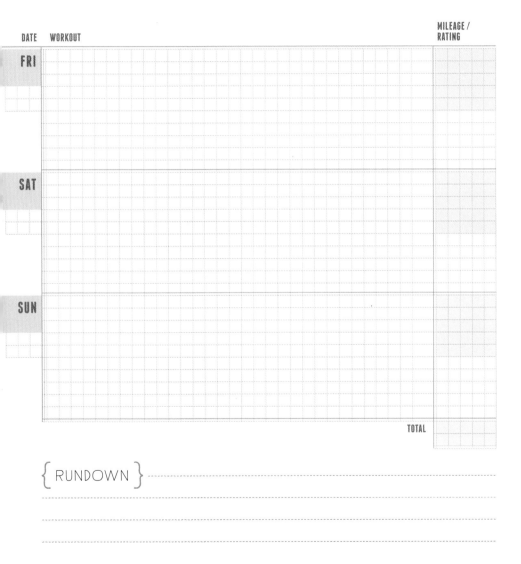

DATE	WORKOUT	MILEAGE / RATING
FRI		
SAT		
SUN		
	TOTAL	

{ RUNDOWN }

THIS WEEK'S FOCUS

Obstacles you might face:

_____

_____

_____

DATE	WORKOUT	MILEAGE / RATING
MON		
TUES		
WED		
THURS		

"I believe the most important single thing, beyond discipline and creativity, is daring to dare." MAYA ANGELOU

DATE	WORKOUT	MILEAGE / RATING
FRI		
SAT		
SUN		
	TOTAL	

{ RUNDOWN }

Strengths you'll need to call on:

DATE	WORKOUT	MILEAGE / RATING
MON		
TUES		
WED		
THURS		

*"Never underestimate the power of dreams and the influence of the human spirit.
We are all the same in this notion: The potential for greatness lives within each of us."*

WILMA RUDOLPH, OLYMPIC CHAMPION & CIVIL RIGHTS PIONEER

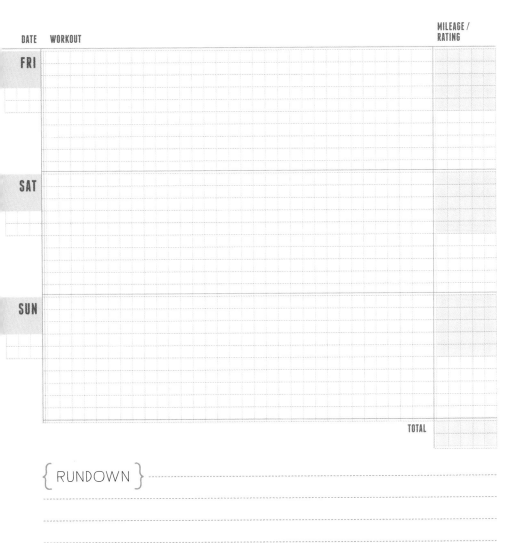

DATE	WORKOUT	MILEAGE / RATING
FRI		
SAT		
SUN		
	TOTAL	

{ RUNDOWN }

THIS WEEK'S FOCUS

Accomplishing your goal will feel like . . .

....

....

....

DATE	WORKOUT	MILEAGE / RATING
MON		
TUES		
WED		
THURS		

"Don't let fear decide your future."
    SHALANE FLANAGAN, OLYMPIC BRONZE MEDALIST

DATE	WORKOUT	MILEAGE / RATING
FRI		
SAT		
SUN		
		TOTAL

{ RUNDOWN }

THIS WEEK'S FOCUS

Changes in your environment that will bring success:

_____

_____

_____

DATE	WORKOUT	MILEAGE / RATING
MON		
TUES		
WED		
THURS		

"To feel ambition and to act upon it is to embrace the unique calling of our souls. Not to act upon that ambition is to turn our backs on ourselves and on the reason for our existence."

STEVEN PRESSFIELD, AUTHOR OF TURNING PRO

DATE	WORKOUT	MILEAGE / RATING
FRI		
SAT		
SUN		
	TOTAL	

{ RUNDOWN }

CHECK-IN HOW I'M DOING . . .

BELIEVE IN GROWTH

MAKE YOUR
MARK

PERSONALITY & PERFORMANCE

There's no such thing as a one-size-fits-all training plan. Even if two people have a lot in common, they can have very different reactions to and perceptions of the same stressor. Some pro athletes fret in advance over all the variables that could affect their training weeks—bad weather or a busy week looms on the horizon, causing worry and what-ifs.

On the other hand, I know pro athletes who barely find time to squeeze in training between all of the other stuff they enjoy doing. It can be stressful or unproductive for these athletes to restrict their lifestyle more exclusively to training. The ideal approach to training, competing, and maintaining a balanced life will—and should—look different for each of us.

Your training plan will be shaped by all of the things that make you unique—lifestyle, personality, and genetics, for starters. Genetics plays more of a role than you might think. Beyond your physical attributes, genetics can determine how you approach your sport. The

processing of dopamine in our prefrontal cortex has been attributed to a single gene, COMT. This gene can determine how you process and deal with stress. In *Top Dog: The Science of Winning*, Po Bronson and Ashley Merryman explain how the two personality types as determined by this COMT gene are referred to as "warriors" and "worriers."

To get a feel for which type best describes you, take our quiz. Knowing your personal strengths and liabilities will help you maximize your ability.

Worriers

Diligent as worker bees, these athletes thrive on routine. Worriers love order

Personality QUIZ

1. Place a check mark next to the statement that is most true.

2. Tally up the check marks in each column. The higher score shows which personality type you lean toward.

WORRIER	WARRIOR
Before races you stress about the competition even if you've beaten them in the past.	Before races you never look at the start lists—whoever shows up, shows up.
It's imperative that you hit your scheduled workout splits no matter what.	You see your training schedule as a rough guide for what needs to be done.
You run the same set of routes you've run for years.	You often seek out new trails and routes. You love exploring new places.
You analyze how you feel in training and before races even if you're hitting your goal times.	You don't think about training or racing much outside of practice.
You remember your (and other athletes') workout times and race results, both recently and in the past.	You rarely remember details and times from past workouts or performances (unless you've kept a training journal).
Your training usually indicates how well your races will go.	You can struggle in training but then feel awesome in races.
You usually know the forecast better than the local weatherperson. A girl needs to know wind speeds and pollen counts.	Your coach gets after you for being too busy and showing up tired for practice.
Your coaches and friends tell you to "be more positive," but there is always something or someone to worry about, and faking "positivity" stresses you out.	If you're worried about something, it usually affects your performances. You like to feel calm and positive before you race.
Some might see your life as quiet and simple, but you like the athlete's life. Rest and recovery are really important to you, and you don't have much energy left for other things.	Your life is hectic at times and can get too busy. You're not one to sit around and wait to run; you have lots of other passions and projects that energize you.

WORRIER	WARRIOR
Your ring finger is shorter than your index finger.	Your ring finger is clearly longer than your index finger.
You approach risks in a methodical way with a solid action plan.	You've always been a bit of a daredevil.
You like to hit your splits even if it means you will lead a race and have to push the pace yourself.	You love to be in a race and watch it unfold while you bide my time before making your move. Finish times are of secondary importance. For you, it's all about the racing.
You're all about details before races—weather, travel delays, competition. You like to be prepared for every possibility.	Delays, weather conditions, competition—they're out of my control, so you don't worry about them.
You like to lie low on your break from training. Anytime you do too much extracurricular stuff, you end up sick or injured.	When the season ends, you are ready to blow off some steam and do lots of fun travel and stuff you don't get to do when training and racing.
You're not sure what else you'd do if I wasn't a runner. Hmmmmm . . .	You have five other ideas for what you would do if you weren't a runner. In fact, you struggle to focus on one interest for too long.
You've learned what training works for you, and you stick to what you know.	You've tried dozens of training philosophies, and you're still not sure exactly what works best for you.
You like routine and usually train at the same time every day.	Routine, schmootine. You run when you find a free minute to get out the door.
Your perfect vacation is an all-inclusive resort that you've been going to for years. Everything is organized, and you hardly have to leave.	My idea of a perfect vacation is traveling to a country whose name I can hardly pronounce with people I've never met and a wide-open agenda.
TOTAL	TOTAL

and are happiest when they have a plan with clear objectives. They tend to fret over the details and analyze all potential outcomes. Worriers can be challenged by stressful situations, but they are persistent and tenacious individuals who learn from their experiences. These traits allow them to be very successful even in high-risk career paths. They're not rattled by negative thinking; in fact, they use it to prepare themselves for worst-case scenarios.

If worry isn't kept in check, it can lead to anxiety disorders. Worriers can sometimes be introverted and rigid in their ways, which causes them to be less open to new people or experiences.

Warriors

These are the quintessential "born-to-be-wild" risk-takers. Warriors are free-spirited and quick to say yes to an adventure. High-stakes, high-pressure situations are where they thrive. They actually need stress in order to achieve optimal cognitive functioning, and they seem to need deadlines to achieve peak focus and mental alertness. Warriors come alive and perform well on race day.

A lack of focus can make it difficult to honor the most meaningful ambitions. While they have no problem rising to the challenge on race day, warriors often struggle with the day-to-day grind. If they fail to prioritize and limit their activity, they'll end up exhausted and fall short of their goals.

While warriors might appear to be primed for success in athletics, worriers often outperform warriors over the long term. Athletes at every level must learn how to maximize their personality type to achieve their goals. Both worriers and warriors can be successful, and best of all, they can complement each other! Worriers keep warriors focused and organized, while warriors liven up the routine and keep things fun. Whatever camp you fall into, you will benefit from adopting a few traits from the other end of the spectrum. ▪️RMD

Tips from USA Champion Molly Huddle

WORRIER

☆ Write out a plan for race day

Include every detail from transportation to meal times. Note important locations and instructions, and list out everything you need to bring along.

☆ Break down your goal

If you are aiming for a specific time, write out the splits for each section of the race. Smaller steps are less intimidating and easier to focus on. If your goal is a specific place or rank, identify a strategy that will help you accomplish it. Identify a competitor who will help you hit the pace you need.

☆ Overcome the worries

Write down your biggest worry or fear. How would you deal with it if it actually happened? Now write over your fear with a positive mantra that you can repeat if the worry creeps back into your mind.

☆ Find time to drop the routine

Take a walk on the wild side every now and then. It's good to get out of your comfort zone and be adventurous (even if only for a few hours). Open up to new experiences that have the potential to broaden your interests and inspire you.

WARRIOR

☆ Partner up

Training partners create synergy and help you tap your competitive nature in training and maybe even mix up the places and races that you run.

☆ Find and stick to a plan that works

Don't be distracted by every new training method, gimmick, or gadget. You might find you need a coach to create a plan and motivate you (or sometimes just straight-up yell at you) in order to get your work done consistently.

☆ Rein in your zest for life

If your life is a series of all-night cram sessions, weekend raves, and drifting around the autobahn, toning it down for a few weeks before a race will help you be rested and ready when it counts.

☆ Let adventures be your reward

Passionate individuals must figure out how to prioritize. Knowing when to give something your full attention and when to kick back and explore will help keep each aspect of life enjoyable.

☆ Take time to pause and reflect

Extracting the lessons from each experience is a proven ingredient for long-term success.

Make a plan for PERSONAL GROWTH

STRENGTHS

BLIND SPOTS

WHAT NEEDS TO CHANGE

THIS WEEK'S FOCUS

You feel strongest when . . .

....

....

....

DATE	WORKOUT	MILEAGE / RATING
MON		
TUES		
WED		
THURS		

"Sometimes you have to push yourself, and it can be uncomfortable. You will want to quit. But if you can find your edge and embrace the discomfort even for a little bit, you'll find a new level of fitness, skill, and knowledge. And there's no better feeling than growth." Roísín McGettigan-Dumas

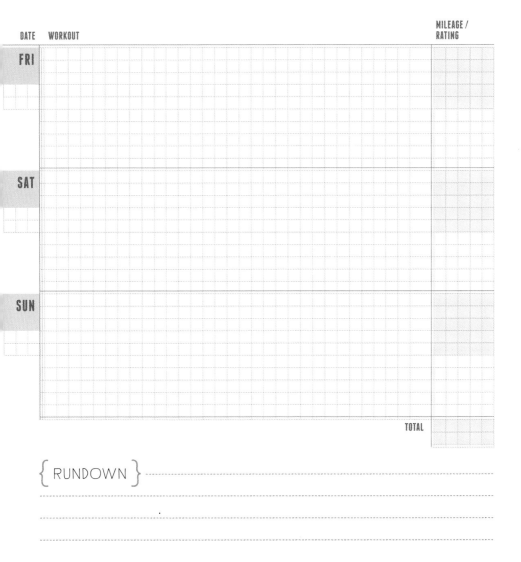

DATE	WORKOUT	MILEAGE / RATING
FRI		
SAT		
SUN		
	TOTAL	

{ RUNDOWN }

THIS WEEK'S FOCUS

What holds you back most?

_____

_____

_____

DATE	WORKOUT	MILEAGE / RATING
MON		
TUES		
WED		
THURS		

"Be like a postage stamp. Stick to one thing until you get there."
            JOSH BILLINGS, HUMORIST

DATE	WORKOUT	MILEAGE / RATING
FRI		
SAT		
SUN		
	TOTAL	

{ RUNDOWN }

THIS WEEK'S FOCUS

No matter what, you'll be satisfied with...

DATE	WORKOUT	MILEAGE / RATING
MON		
TUES		
WED		
THURS		

"Joy lies in the fight, in the attempt, in the suffering involved, not in the victory itself."

MAHATMA GANDHI

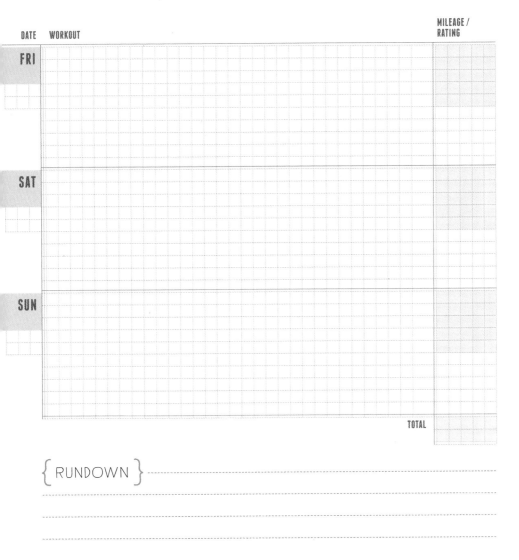

DATE	WORKOUT	MILEAGE / RATING
FRI		
SAT		
SUN		
	TOTAL	

{ RUNDOWN }

Whom do you admire and why?

DATE	WORKOUT	MILEAGE / RATING
MON		
TUES		
WED		
THURS		

"My philosophy on running is, I don't dwell on it, I do it."
    JOAN BENOIT SAMUELSON, FIRST WOMEN'S OLYMPIC MARATHON CHAMPION

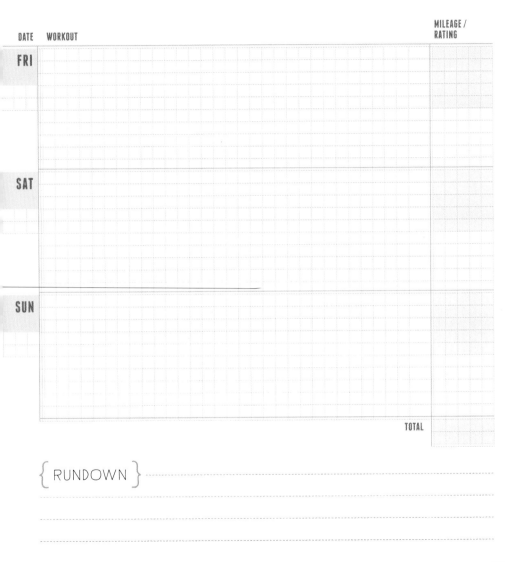

DATE	WORKOUT	MILEAGE / RATING
FRI		
SAT		
SUN		
	TOTAL	

{ RUNDOWN }

CHECK-IN HOW I'M DOING . . .

BELIEVE IN YOUR TRAINING PROGRAM

I don't need to tell you that training your body is important. Runners tend to overlook some of the practices that support training—mental training, or nutrition, or sleep—but everyone knows you need to train your body to be a good runner. As for how you do it, there is no end to the ways.

When I went pro, I traveled all over the world and met incredibly successful athletes trained by different coaches and was shocked to find that we all trained differently. Some people worked out hard two times a week, some four times a week. Some focused on tempo runs with speed; some slammed long, hard intervals twice a week. Some did periodized training with months and months of high mileage; some touched on speed work year-round. Some lifted heavy weights, some light, some not at all. Some kept track of miles; others counted minutes. Some hardly tracked anything at all.

About 10 years ago a sister in sport from New Zealand, Kim Smith, helped me make sense of it all. That particular summer we were based in Belgium, and we became close friends. At the time, our race performances were really similar, but that's about where the similarities ended. Well, that and our love for chocolate, coffee, and books. As roommates for races in Italy, Finland, and more, we spent hours talking about training. I tried hard to get in my veggies. Kim seemed to survive on bacon and gummy bears (not anymore). My hard workout days were preceded by a 45-minute warm-up of jogging, drills, stretching, and listening to the theme song from *Rocky*. Kim seemed to just roll out of bed and suffer through it. She could grind out repeat miles at paces I could only dream about. I could switch gears and move in more powerfully athletic ways. At the end of the day, we both got the job done, and we raced within seconds of one another. She has since moved up to the marathon distance and become one of the most successful women in the history of the sport.

The fact that variation exists between training programs doesn't rule out best practices or themes that correlate with success. A training plan is like a recipe for making a pot of chili. It's the kind of meal where a guide is likely to be more useful than a formula. Tomatoes, meat, beans (or not), spices . . . maybe some veggies . . . There are countless ways to make chili. And, yeah, you can definitely screw up chili, but you can also have a chili cook-off with a hundred different varieties and come away having enjoyed most of them. So don't waste too much time comparing yourself with or copying other people. **LF**

Components of a Successful Training Plan

- ☆ Begins with your PRs, goals, and strengths/weaknesses in mind
- ☆ Builds toward one to three key races
- ☆ Grows out of an overarching philosophy or method rooted in science and experience
- ☆ Works different energy systems: aerobic, threshold, anaerobic, speed
- ☆ Incorporates your favorite types of workouts to feed your joy of the sport
- ☆ Builds in adequate recovery
- ☆ Flexes to accommodate your health, other commitments, etc.
- ☆ Has momentum, building complexity, difficulty, and confidence over time
- ☆ Rarely asks you to do things you can't achieve
- ☺ Is fun. At least most of the time!

One last thing. A training plan is completely useless without belief. Be mindful about your training: Don't be afraid to ask questions or educate yourself, but be careful not to overanalyze. If you are studying the bark of a tree with a magnifying glass, there's no way for you to see the whole forest. Step back a bit and start enjoying the scenery, the ground beneath your feet, and the wind on your face.

WORKOUTS

THE GO-TO FARTLEK

15 min. warm-up jog

1 min. on, 2 min. off, 2 min. on, 1 min. off

Repeat fartlek set 4–6 times

15 min. cooldown jog

Fartlek means "speed play" in Swedish, and it is a staple for learning to "run by feel" instead of being obsessed with pace or distance. The fartlek is a continuous run— during the ons you crank it up a bit, and during the offs you slow to your typical easy run pace.

This workout is perfect for when you're coming off something—an illness, a season break, a recently healed injury. Or, when you're bored of "just running."

THE OMG

1 mi. hard, 1200 harder, 800 harder still, 400 whatever's left!

5–7 min. walking or slow jogging recovery between each interval

This workout is not for the faint of heart. It's for when you really want to smash one, when you have a good base of training behind you and when you don't have a race coming up for a few weeks. Each interval is very challenging but not quite all-out, and you should plan it so you can go 1–3 seconds faster per lap on the following interval.

THE STRENGTH LADDER

400, 800, 1200, 1 mi., 1 mi., 1200, 800, 400

2–3 min. rest between each interval

The paces get easier as the intervals get longer, and then they get gradually faster again on the way back down the ladder.

Wanna do it by time instead of distance? Try this variation:

2 min., 3 min., 4 min., 5 min., 5 min., 4 min., 3 min., 2 min.

2–3 min. rest between each interval

THE BITER

6 × 400 with 1 min. rest between each interval
Recover 3–5 minutes between sets

6 × 300 with 45 sec. rest between each interval
Recover 3–5 minutes between sets

6 × 200 with 30 sec. rest between each interval

This track workout is called the biter because as you get to #5 and #6 of each set, the lactic acid starts to "bite" and it becomes difficult to relax and maintain your form. This works on speed endurance, which is your ability to tolerate faster paces with shorter recoveries. This type of workout is the secret sauce of the world's best milers, and it teaches you to relax into discomfort rather than fight it, which is good for milers and marathoners alike! The (extremely short) recoveries are walking or standing during the sets, and the set rest is a slow lap walk/jog.

THE PRE-RACE BLOWOUT

2 mi. tempo, 800 at 10K pace, 2 mi. tempo

2 min. rest between each interval

Pro marathoner Stephanie Rothstein Bruce uses this workout three days before all her big races and recommends it for all the recreational athletes that use her coaching program, "Running with the Bruces." The tempo is somewhere between marathon and half-marathon pace. The 800 is strong and challenging, which opens up the body, heart, and lungs, making the final 2-mile tempo effort feel like a breeze in comparison.

THE ROWLAND TEMPO

3 × 9 min. progressive tempo run (3/3/3)

1–2 min. recovery between intervals

A standard tempo run involves picking a comfortably hard pace for 4–8 miles that allows you to speak in short sentences, but there are some nice flourishes you can add that will help you improve and make tempos more interesting. By flirting with efforts slightly below, at, and slightly above tempo effort, you can nudge yourself onto a new level!

During a 9-minute tempo, you gradually increase the pace every 3 minutes, running 3 minutes a little slower than tempo, 3 minutes at tempo, and 3 minutes a little faster than tempo. Rest 1–2 minutes, then repeat that two more times. Over several weeks, try building up this workout from 3/3/3 to 4/4/4 and 5/5/5.

HILL CUT-DOWNS

Find a nice, long hill, preferably in a residential neighborhood where there isn't much traffic. Get in 15–20 minutes of easy running first, then:

- **4 × 1:30 min. hill controlled, jog-down recovery**
- **4 × 60 sec. hill strong, jog-down recovery**
- **4 × 30 sec. hill very strong, walk-down recovery**
- **4 × 15 sec. hill 100% effort, walk-down recovery**

Hill repeats are similar to lifting weights when it comes to building power and strength. Form is very important. Think about your foot landing underneath your body and using your butt muscles powerfully to propel you forward, rather than your foot landing in front of you and dragging your body up and over it. Keep your spine straight and a slight forward lean at the waist as you drive your elbows back and bring your hands up no higher than your collarbone. Imagine your body as a spring. If you bounce a spring on the ground, it will bounce back up. If there is a kink or sag in the spring, it will bounce off course or, worse yet, not bounce much at all. Stack your spine and keep your core nice and strong and you will get the most out of your power up the hills!

THE SNEAKY

90-min. run on hilly terrain, preferably a trail that's winding and makes you concentrate on your footing without being too dangerous

A long, hilly run is a sneaky workout that ticks all the boxes. Let the terrain dictate your effort, and when you're done you'll have done your long run, tempo, and interval work all at once. Plan an easy day or two afterward!

THE STANFORD STANDARD

6–8 × 1K at 5K pace or slightly slower

2:30 min. rest between intervals

This workout is designed to help you find your rhythm for a 5K race and learn to tolerate some discomfort. As you get in better shape, first shorten the recoveries (no shorter than 1 minute) before speeding up the paces. Start out smart, and make the last one your best one, always, just like a race well run.

If you've shortened the recoveries and speeded up the paces and want to take the next step, try the marathoner version by Stephanie Rothstein Bruce:

THE HEAVY LEGS

10–15 × 1K at marathon pace

1 min. rest between intervals

"By the last couple, the recovery feels so short and your legs so heavy that you're thinking, *No way can I do this*, but then you push through, and you leave feeling so confident that you can handle the last 6 miles of the marathon."

THE POWER STATION

6 mi. run with 8 × 30 sec. sprint set (95% effort) at halfway point

Walk-down recovery

As part of a 6-miler, find a reasonably steep hill somewhere in the middle of the run and begin the 30-second hill sprints.

TIP: You don't have to look at your watch the whole time. After the first 30-second sprint, leave a landmark at your finish line (T-shirt, water bottle, stick) and try to match or beat that mark for the rest of the workout!

THE OREGON

5 × 400 at 5K pace

200 float recovery between intervals

1 lap jog recovery

1K at 5K pace

1 lap jog recovery

5 × 400 at 5K pace

200 float recovery between intervals

A variation of this workout was reportedly done under coach Bill Bowerman at the University of Oregon back in the day. Legendary coach Vin Lananna made this a staple for his distance runners for many years. Try to run the 400s smoothly at 5K pace, then transition right into a 200 meter float, which is a slow run (but not a shuffle), and then go right back into a quick 400, and so on. The next interval is a 1K at 5K pace; then, after recovering, you go straight back into another set of 5 × 400 with 200 float.

KENYAN PROGRESSION RUN

30–60 min. run, increasing speed each mi. by 10–15 sec.

Kenyans are known for starting out runs at a shuffle and then gradually chipping down the pace. Work your way down to a pace that makes it difficult to speak in long sentences by the end, similar to a tempo run. This is a good workout to fit into the middle of your week, so long as it doesn't butt up against a hard workout.

Something new you'd like to try in training:

....

....

....

DATE	WORKOUT	MILEAGE / RATING
MON		
TUES		
WED		
THURS		

*"I ran and ran and ran every day, and I acquired this sense of determination,
this sense of spirit that I would never, never give up, no matter what else happened."*

WILMA RUDOLPH, OLYMPIC CHAMPION & CIVIL RIGHTS PIONEER

DATE	WORKOUT	MILEAGE / RATING
FRI		
SAT		
SUN		
	TOTAL	

{ RUNDOWN }

THIS WEEK'S FOCUS

The strongest parts of your preparation:

_____
_____
_____

DATE	WORKOUT	MILEAGE / RATING
MON		
TUES		
WED		
THURS		

"The greats weren't great because at birth they could paint; the greats were great because they paint a lot."

MACKLEMORE, RAPPER

DATE	WORKOUT	MILEAGE / RATING
FRI		
SAT		
SUN		
	TOTAL	

{ RUNDOWN }

THIS WEEK'S FOCUS

You're consistent when it comes to . . .

DATE	WORKOUT	MILEAGE / RATING
MON		
TUES		
WED		
THURS		

"Erase from your mind that your preparation must be perfect. Hard work + dedication = a shot at your dreams. Keep believing." KARA GOUCHER, WORLD CHAMPIONSHIPS BRONZE MEDALIST

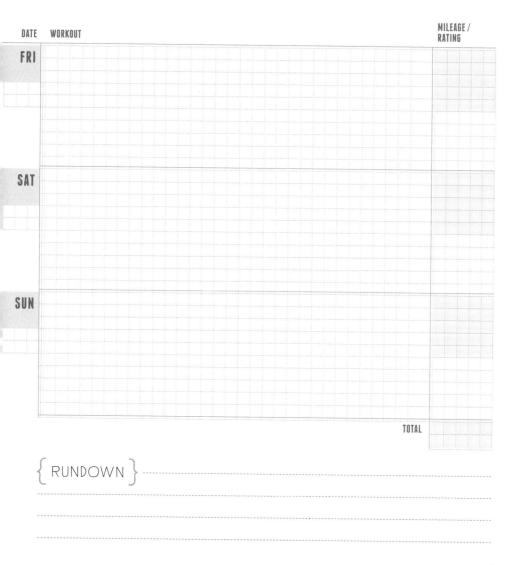

DATE	WORKOUT	MILEAGE / RATING
FRI		
SAT		
SUN		
	TOTAL	

{ RUNDOWN }

THIS WEEK'S FOCUS

When it gets hard, you'll tell yourself...

	DATE	WORKOUT	MILEAGE / RATING
MON			
TUES			
WED			
THURS			

"It's amazing how the same pace in practice can feel so much harder than on race day. Stay confident. Trust the process."   SARA HALL, PRO RUNNER & COFOUNDER OF THE HALL STEPS FOUNDATION

DATE	WORKOUT	MILEAGE / RATING
FRI		
SAT		
SUN		
	TOTAL	

{ RUNDOWN }

Recently you've improved at . . .

....

....

....

DATE	WORKOUT	MILEAGE / RATING
MON		
TUES		
WED		
THURS		

"Look for little improvements every day."
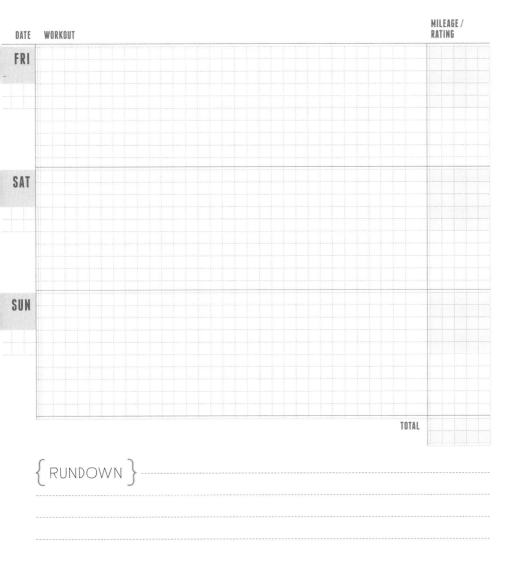
COACH RAY TREACY, DIRECTOR OF CROSS-COUNTRY & TRACK OPERATIONS AT PROVIDENCE COLLEGE

DATE	WORKOUT	MILEAGE / RATING
FRI		
SAT		
SUN		
	TOTAL	

{ RUNDOWN }

CHECK-IN HOW I'M DOING . . .

BELIEVE IN YOUR COURAGE

FACE *your* FOE

MEET RESISTANCE

Your mind plays a big role in performance. It's normal for negative thoughts to creep in at various points in your training, but if you're not careful, they will stand in the way of your goals. Best-selling author Steven Pressfield calls these self-sabotaging thoughts "Resistance." The spiritual guru Eckhart Tolle calls the critical voice in our heads "the ego." Wall Street bankers call it "FUD" (fear, uncertainty, doubt).

Call them what you like, these thoughts are notorious for holding you back and limiting your performance.

In all my years of competing, both nationally and internationally, my biggest and most devastating competitor was Resistance. Before I learned effective coping strategies, Resistance frequently showed up on race day and sabotaged everything I had worked so hard to achieve. I would train all year for a chance to prove myself in a big race only to wind up fearful, tense, and miserable, performing well below my ability.

Great Britain's Olympic team psychiatrist Steve Peters describes our instinctual response to Resistance as the "chimp brain." When fear and doubt are activated, we regress to a primitive state of mind. It is possible to develop mental toughness that will override this pea-sized fear-inducing part of the brain and manage it proactively. We talk about some of those tactics in the Head Games sidebar on pages 120–21.

Resistance affects everyone differently, but it leaves no one out. At some point in the course of your journey as an athlete, you will perform below your potential and blame yourself for the outcome. In these situations, it's essential to keep two things in mind: (1) Everyone who dares to chase her dreams experiences moments like this, and (2) Resistance can never be permanently defeated.

View Resistance as a test of your will. By embracing it as a necessary part of the journey to reach your goals, you escape its powerful grip and free yourself to focus on the work you need to do. RMD

Athlete Enemy #1: Resistance

She's your inner critic. She will ruin your best intentions, pull you into negative self talk, give you plenty of excuses, and leave you mired in doubt. From the moment you set your goals and throughout your training and racing, you will be on her radar. Procrastination, drama, distraction, fear of failure, and indecision all play to her strengths, so if you want to prevail, you will need to keep these in check.

You are not the only one she's gunning for. Anyone with aspirations, from novice to pro, is her target, and overly passionate, self-conscious people are most vulnerable.

Focusing on your goals will keep you on the right track. Build up consistent training, sticking to your program. Develop mental fortitude and resilience and you will toe the line with confidence, knowing that Resistance cannot defeat you.

DO IT **IT'S TOO HARD** YOU ARE
LATER *Eat another cookie* TOO SLOW
IF ONLY YOU HAD WHAT SHE HAS
Quit now **YOU CAN'T START TOMORROW** IT'S
YOU'RE TOO OLD YOU WON'T TOO FAR
Skip practice MAKE IT You can't keep up

10-Minute WEED REMOVAL

Like a garden, our minds need tending. Negative thoughts are weeds—destructive, crowding out positive thoughts and making us feel out of control. Use this exercise weekly, or whenever you need to weed out the negativity and regain peace of mind.

NEGATIVE THOUGHTS

1. Set a timer for five minutes. Write down all your negative thoughts, even if they sound irrational. When the timer beeps, stop.

2. Take three deep belly breaths. Now look back at what you wrote. Identify negative chatter, or Resistance, that is sabotaging your confidence.

3. Write a rational rebuttal for each negative thought. Build a case for yourself point by point.

Every time a negative thought steals your attention, be mindful of it and replace it with a rational, positive thought. Change the conversation and move forward.

POSITIVE REBUTTALS

Need more help? *Many problems are solved when aired on a run with sisters in sport. When you can't get perspective on your emotional drama, someone else's viewpoint is helpful. If the weeds continue to rage out of control, seek out a professional counselor or psychologist.*

A good example of your resilience:

....

....

....

DATE	WORKOUT	MILEAGE / RATING
MON		
TUES		
WED		
THURS		

"Most people can't handle adversity. Simply by not quitting, you'll succeed."

STEPHANIE ROTHSTEIN BRUCE, PRO MARATHONER & COFOUNDER OF PICKY BARS

DATE	WORKOUT	MILEAGE / RATING
FRI		
SAT		
SUN		
	TOTAL	

{ RUNDOWN }

What "pain" (sacrifice) are you willing to endure?

DATE	WORKOUT	MILEAGE / RATING
MON		
TUES		
WED		
THURS		

"When you're a dreamer, heartbreak and failure come with the territory. But I can tell you it's worth it because it's a way of living that is both moving and memorable." LAUREN FLESHMAN

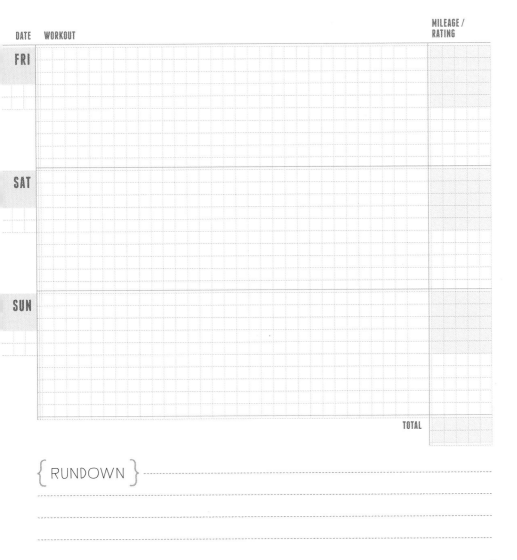

DATE	WORKOUT	MILEAGE / RATING
FRI		
SAT		
SUN		
	TOTAL	

{ RUNDOWN }

What holds you back?

....

....

....

DATE	WORKOUT	MILEAGE / RATING
MON		
TUES		
WED		
THURS		

*"You can find evidence to support anything you believe about yourself.
So you might as well believe you can achieve your most outlandish goals."*

JULIE SYGIEL, CHEMICAL ENGINEER & ENTREPRENEUR, FOUNDER OF DEAR KATE

DATE	WORKOUT	MILEAGE / RATING
FRI		
SAT		
SUN		
	TOTAL	

{ RUNDOWN }

THIS WEEK'S FOCUS

A visual cue to summon when you feel weak:

....

....

....

DATE	WORKOUT	MILEAGE / RATING
MON		
TUES		
WED		
THURS		

"Mental will is a muscle that needs exercise, just like the muscles of the body."
      LYNN JENNINGS, THREE-TIME WORLD CROSS-COUNTRY CHAMPION

DATE	WORKOUT	MILEAGE / RATING
FRI		
SAT		
SUN		
	TOTAL	

{ RUNDOWN }

CHECK-IN HOW I'M DOING ...

BELIEVE IN YOUR DIET

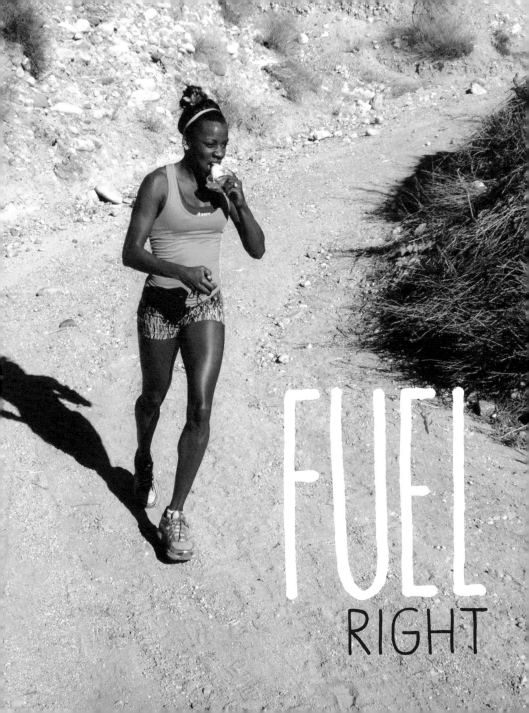

FUEL
RIGHT

FEED THE MACHINE

Lauren

Establishing good habits around what and when you eat can shape your body into a performance machine. It sounds simple, but in practice nutrition is a socially and emotionally loaded subject that carries pretty big consequences if you get it wrong.

For an athlete, the best approach is to become informed about healthy eating and healthy ways to gain or lose weight without allowing nutrition to control your life or surpass your focus on performance.

If you can become an ace at nutrition, you will reap the benefits:

+ **Feel better all over.** Food is fuel, and filling your tank with premium will help you get the most out of your body without bonking, getting stomachaches, or feeling fatigued. At the very least, you won't feel like doo-doo all the time.

+ **Recover faster.** For elites, speed of recovery is crucial to being able to handle a world-class training load.

(Bonus: You'll be able to maintain a social life with coherent conversations while training.)

+ **Shape your body for better performance.** Learn how to lose or gain weight without a lot of drama or stress.

In truth, good nutrition is easier said than done. We all grow up with different habits based on our home environment and the behavior that is modeled for us by parents and friends. At some point after puberty, usually when we move out on our own for the first time, our bodies start changing and we suddenly realize that we can't just eat whatever we want whenever we want. So there we stand, at a junction in the road with countless options and no obvious direction. Which nutritional path we choose is influenced by culture, social behaviors, education, and luck. Most of us look to friends or teammates for which path to take, most of whom will direct us to places we don't want to go. Wherever you are now, you can always decide to stop, learn, and change direction. The difficult part is finding reliable directions that allow you to proceed with confidence.

It wasn't until college that I realized I would have to watch what I ate in order to maintain a healthy body built for performance. After I gained the freshman 15, adjustments had to be made, but losing weight was a terrifying prospect. Around me were examples of women who, once they flicked on that switch to caring about food, developed eating habits that ate away at their bodies and their minds. Their obsession with weight and food created performance peaks and pitfalls, along with intense team strife. It seemed incredibly hard for them to turn the switch back off.

And then there were other women whose bodies didn't fluctuate much. They ate normally, and they seemed to have no problem getting into race shape when it mattered. Were they just born with an incredible metabolism? Or was

it something else? After training with them and observing their habits, I noticed that they shared a few things in common:

* Good eating habits, by way of educating themselves on the topic or by relying on positive habits they brought from home
* Lack of emotion about food; not motivated much by social eating
* Good self-control, with room for indulgences in moderation
* Fairly habitual, moderately scheduled eating; they had their go-to foods and then went on about their day

As a social eater with poor self-control who never paid attention to the "why" of the good food my mama made me, I knew it wouldn't be easy, but I wanted good habits and the mental freedom these women enjoyed around food. It was harder than I thought. Learning new things involves a pretty standard pattern of adoption, at least for me:

* Mind-blown at all the information and science I didn't know existed!
* Absolutely horrified at some of the things I've been doing for years!
* Highly motivated to make changes.

* Paying attention to every single thing all of a sudden.
* Realizing I'm on the edge of over-doing it, or maybe even just did . . .
* Stepping back from the ledge and finding a happy balance.

Whether it is learning about nutrition, climate change, or anything else, my reaction is pretty much the same—I dive in. But with passion comes the risk of overdoing it. With climate change, the overdone scenario is that I go off the grid and pull apart my entire lifestyle because I'm obsessed with my carbon footprint, but with nutrition and body weight, the consequences of taking it too far could destroy my physical health and my relationship with food for the rest of my life.

I am one of the lucky ones. I came close enough to the edge of the cliff to see the view down there and then safely stepped back. Not everyone is so lucky. What I've learned about nutrition in 11-plus years of experience as a professional athlete is that it is not only possible but crucial to address nutrition in a healthy way. The key is to create some healthy guidelines that give you results without taking over your mind. When you free your mind from food issues and put that energy into training and racing, you just might find that your body weight takes care of itself. **LF**

Warning Signs You Might Need to Adjust Your Path

✗ Your social life is negatively impacted by your diet.

✗ You develop habits you feel you need to hide in public. If you wouldn't do it in front of other people, you probably shouldn't be doing it.

✗ Your day is ruined if the number on the scale isn't what you want or if you stray from your meal plan.

✗ You care more about looking fit than competing well.

✗ You become a food pusher, making or buying sweets you won't eat and pushing them on others.

✗ You skip several periods in a row.

Lauren's Top Nutrition Tips

✳ Eat 200 calories within 15–30 minutes of exercise

This rule has been the single best influence on my performance and physique. There's plenty of science to show that during that post-exercise window, a balanced snack is absorbed right into the glycogen stores—not your fat stores—and helps your muscles recover. It also takes the edge off your hunger so that you are able to make healthier choices at your next meal. *If you do only one thing, do this.*

✳ Eat foods as close to the source as possible

The fewer steps of processing a food goes through, the better.

✳ Workouts are not the time to skimp on calories or carbohydrates

Inadequate fueling right before, during, and immediately after exercise slows your metabolism and makes you more likely to hoard calories when you do eat them. Those extreme hunger fluctuations have negative effects on hormonal health. If you find yourself binge-eating late at night, it's a clear sign that you need to eat more fuel surrounding exercise.

✳ Don't overthink meals

When it's mealtime, a good general guide is to have one-quarter of your plate covered with quality protein, one-quarter with a minimally processed whole-grain carbohydrate source, and one-half with veggies and/or fruit.

✳ Calorie counting is no way to live

It helps the clueless find their bearings, but it should only be temporary. Reading nutrition labels can help you get a handle on assembling balanced meals and setting appropriate portion sizes, but once you figure out some general guidelines for yourself, set yourself free from the numbers.

✳ You don't have to be perfect

A consistent B+ diet gives you great results and leaves room for life (aka chocolate) to happen. Sugar and fat cravings are part of our biology. Even the fastest, fittest runners in the world enjoy treats. You should see how many spoonfuls of sugar the world-champion Kenyans put in their tea!

THIS WEEK'S FOCUS

Ways you can improve your nutritional approach:

DATE	WORKOUT	MILEAGE / RATING
MON		
TUES		
WED		
THURS		

*"Running is about more than just putting one foot in front of the other;
it is about our lifestyle and who we are."*

JOAN BENOIT SAMUELSON, *FIRST WOMEN'S OLYMPIC MARATHON CHAMPION*

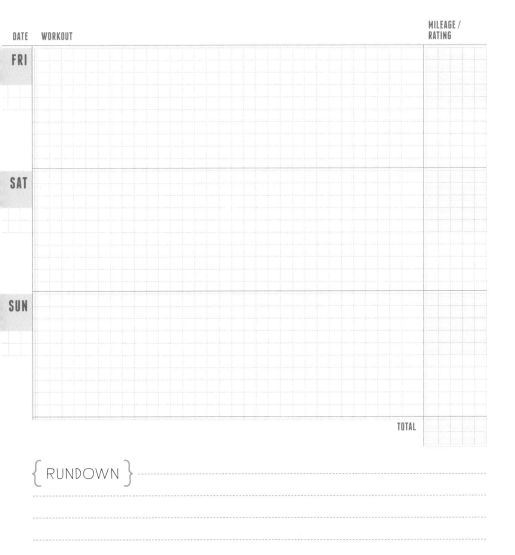

DATE	WORKOUT		MILEAGE / RATING
FRI			
SAT			
SUN			
		TOTAL	

{ RUNDOWN }

THIS WEEK'S FOCUS

What do you want your body to do for you?

DATE	WORKOUT	MILEAGE / RATING
MON		
TUES		
WED		
THURS		

"My motivation waxes and wanes just like anyone else's. But unless I'm pushing myself physically, I feel less than complete. I had many years with near zero attention to my own body, and I felt like I inhabited the earth less. I was less feisty."

DR. SARAH LESKO, FAMILY PHYSICIAN & MOTHER OF THREE BOYS

DATE	WORKOUT	MILEAGE / RATING
FRI		
SAT		
SUN		
	TOTAL	

{ RUNDOWN }

THIS WEEK'S FOCUS

Ideal meal that makes you feel healthy and strong:

....

....

....

DATE	WORKOUT	MILEAGE / RATING
MON		
TUES		
WED		
THURS		

"The life span of a muscle cell is about six months. That means six months from now, your muscles will be completely new. They will form to the demands you put on them and be composed of the things you put into your mouth between now and then. We literally are what we eat."

LAUREN FLESHMAN

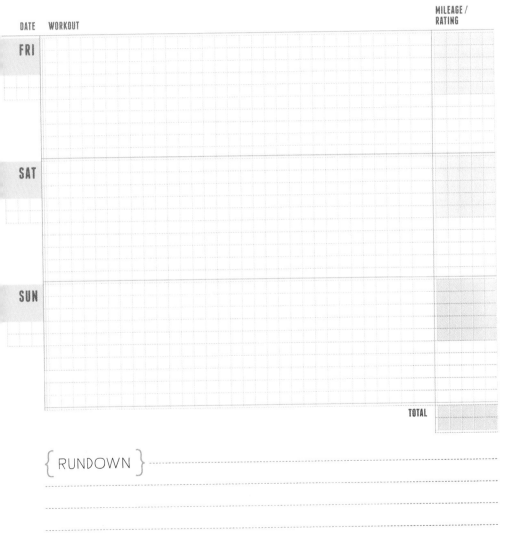

DATE	WORKOUT	MILEAGE / RATING
FRI		
SAT		
SUN		
	TOTAL	

{ RUNDOWN }

THIS WEEK'S FOCUS

Ideal treat to reward yourself:

DATE	WORKOUT	MILEAGE / RATING
MON		
TUES		
WED		
THURS		

"Everything in moderation! Sometimes a cookie makes everything better!"

AMY RUDOLPH, TWO-TIME OLYMPIAN

DATE	WORKOUT	MILEAGE / RATING
FRI		
SAT		
SUN		
	TOTAL	

{ RUNDOWN }

THIS WEEK'S FOCUS

How you will improve your recovery nutrition:

_____

_____

_____

DATE	WORKOUT	MILEAGE / RATING
MON		
TUES		
WED		
THURS		

"Don't try to rush progress. Remember—a step forward, no matter how small, is a step in the right direction." — KARA GOUCHER, *WORLD CHAMPIONSHIPS BRONZE MEDALIST*

DATE	WORKOUT	MILEAGE / RATING
FRI		
SAT		
SUN		
	TOTAL	

{ RUNDOWN }

CHECK-IN HOW I'M DOING . . .

BELIEVE IN YOUR BODY

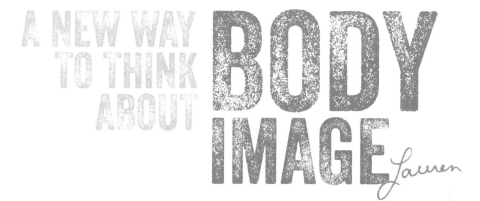

A NEW WAY TO THINK ABOUT BODY IMAGE — Lauren

On the surface it seems quite simple. We have a body. We use this body to go places, do things, hug people, accessorize, create art, give life. Awesome, right? Yeah, sure, but we want to maximize this body. And that's when things get complicated.

The way our culture operates, without having to forage for your own food and all that, it can be pretty hard work to maintain the body you want. And we are surrounded with unrealistic images of what we *should* look like. So most of us spend a lot of time looking in the mirror, setting fitness and diet goals, and then looking in the mirror some more.

In the sport of running, you run faster when you aren't carrying around a bunch of extra weight. It's basic physics. As a pro runner focused on performance, I often have to make changes to my body to get where I want to be. But this process of changing the body is emotionally complex.

As a teenager I spent a lot of time looking at bodies in magazines and on television. In college I spent energy trying to maximize my own body. And in my early 20s I found myself hating parts of my body that refused to change—the parts of me that were hardwired, that didn't fit this or that "ideal." After talking with thousands of runners from around the world, I am now convinced that this is the most common struggle we face as female athletes, and the number-one thing keeping us from our potential. It is not our bodies holding us back but how we view our bodies, whether we choose to love or hate them.

We all struggle with body image at some point, in some capacity. For some it is limited to occasional mirror-scowling, while others find themselves trapped in a cycle of severe body destruction and psychological devastation. Wherever you fall on this spectrum, body image is something every runner needs to prioritize. The bottom line: We all need to develop the skills to love ourselves more, no matter which way the breeze is blowing that particular day.

When it comes time to make changes in our bodies, we need to set ourselves up for success, not just on the scale or in the mirror but in our minds. We can all get results, but at what cost? The most common mistake we make in trying to change our bodies is to be spurred into action by self-loathing. Getting down on yourself might serve as a catalyst to get started, but it doesn't lead to lasting change. Your body might evolve, but your mind will remain stuck. You haven't won until you love the body you're in. **LF**

A 4-Step Plan to Loving Your Body

Long-term change has to start from a place of self-love, not self-loathing. It's a frame of mind. So what is an appropriate way to approach change?

1 Forget the words *skinny* or *thin*. For an athlete, those words imply weakness, fragility, the inability to stand firm in a storm. Strive to make your body more "athletic" — healthy, strong, and built to thrive. An athletic body can take many shapes.

2 Think about what you want your body to do for you rather than what you want to remove from it. Honor your body; don't talk crap about it.

3 Appreciate the variety of body shapes performing well, and select a role model with a body type similar to yours. There are parts of your body that are genetically hardwired and parts you can change. Learn the difference. Any moment dwelling on the unchangeable is a moment wasted.

4 Limit your exposure to negative body imagery. The mind is fertile ground, and it is your responsibility to keep the weeds out. Unfollow that Twitter feed. Unsubscribe to that magazine. Stop watching that stupid TV show. Don't even waste your breath bitching about the destructive nature of these images and messages. Instead, create, seek out, and share the sources that are doing it right.

You respect your one and only body by . . .

_____

_____

_____

DATE	WORKOUT	MILEAGE / RATING
MON		
TUES		
WED		
THURS		

"Shift from thinking to feeling—feel yourself accomplishing your goal. Take that feeling out of your head and put it into your heart. Embrace it as the reality."

ERIN TAYLOR, FOUNDER & HEAD COACH OF JASYOGA

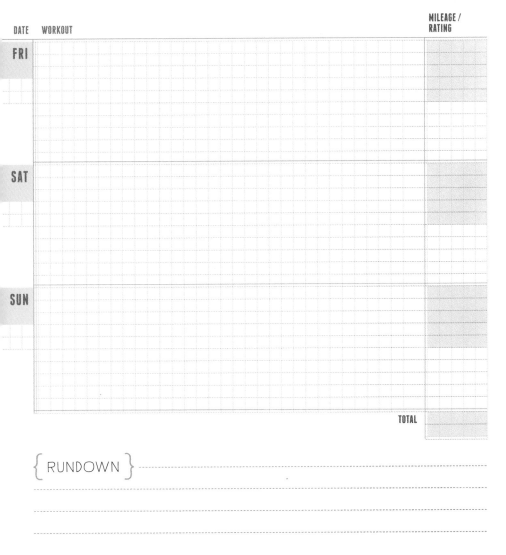

DATE	WORKOUT	MILEAGE / RATING
FRI		
SAT		
SUN		
	TOTAL	

{ RUNDOWN }

THIS WEEK'S FOCUS

This negative body thought is no longer welcome:

....

....

....

DATE	WORKOUT	MILEAGE / RATING
MON		
TUES		
WED		
THURS		

"Spend your mental energy not worrying about body image and redirect it to developing a strong mind. You will need this if you are going to be a force to be reckoned with!"

SARAH JAMIESON, OLYMPIAN & COMMONWEALTH GAMES SILVER MEDALIST

DATE	WORKOUT	MILEAGE / RATING
FRI		
SAT		
SUN		
	TOTAL	

{ RUNDOWN }

Something you love about your body:

....

....

....

DATE	WORKOUT	MILEAGE / RATING
MON		
TUES		
WED		
THURS		

"There's not one body type that equates to success. Accept the body you have and be the best you can be with it." MARY CULLEN, NCAA CHAMPION & EUROPEAN CHAMPIONSHIPS MEDALIST

DATE	WORKOUT	MILEAGE / RATING
FRI		
SAT		
SUN		
	TOTAL	

{ RUNDOWN }

Someone you admire who shares your body type:

DATE	WORKOUT		MILEAGE / RATING
MON			
TUES			
WED			
THURS			

"In high school and college I remember seeing really thin, fit, veiny-looking runners and wondering, *Why don't I look like that? They must train more than me.* When I started beating them I realized what matters are the heart, lungs, healthy muscles, and busy mitochondria on the inside that you can't see." MOLLY HUDDLE, USA CHAMPION & AMERICAN-RECORD HOLDER

DATE	WORKOUT	MILEAGE / RATING
FRI		
SAT		
SUN		
	TOTAL	

{ RUNDOWN }

CHECK-IN HOW I'M DOING . . .

BELIEVE IN YOUR EFFORT & HARD WORK

RISE TO THE CHALLENGE

Ever wonder what compels millions of us to lace up our shoes to race on the weekends? The word *competition* is derived from the Latin word *competere*, which means "to come together to seek." Competing in races enables us to seek something we can't get in training alone.

The phenomenon of being watched causes an influx of biological and psychological reactions in the body that have been proven to elevate performance. In my own training, I was always amazed at how hard running specific race paces would be in workouts. I would think, *How am I supposed to tie these reps together for 5K?!* But the mind and body react to competition, tapping hidden reserves of energy, increasing our problem-solving ability and creativity.

Competition can also hinder performance if you are not properly mentally prepared. A flood of naturally occurring hormones primes the body to compete, but these same hormones can also increase negative mental chatter, moodiness, and irritability (think of it as the physiological manifestation of Resistance). Without proper coping mechanisms, this can lead to overstimu-lation and extreme nervousness, both of which decrease the body's ability to perform, however physically prepared it might be. Here are some strategies to get your best results in competition:

Flip the Fear

Over the course of my career, I often felt the weight of the task at hand when I was competing. Thoughts like *You're representing your country—everyone is watching!* and *You better race well—your career depends on it!* would fill my head. It wasn't until later in my career that I really understood the mind-body connection—how an athlete views a competition affects her body's physiology. When you view a race as a threatening situation, your blood flow, lung capacity, and energy levels decrease. As I matured, I learned that reframing competitions as a positive challenge opened the door for my body to benefit from the competitive environment.

I began to experience increased energy production, enthusiasm, and focus (see list below). Instead of thinking of key races as the lion's den, I looked at them as the party of the year, something I could honestly look forward to.

Once I changed my perspective, I began to have more fun, enjoy the performances, and reach my full potential in high-pressure situations.

Find Your Flow

Many top athletes put as much emphasis on their mental preparation before a race as their physical training. And just like physical training, there's no one-size-fits-all approach. It's up to you to find your individual zone of optimal functioning, or IZOF, as sports psychologists like to call it. It's a sweet spot where all of the work you've put in bears fruit.

Some athletes like to be around family and friends before a race; others prefer to be alone. Some listen to certain pump-up songs; others relax with a guided meditation. Finding a strategy that works for you can be just as important as the rest of your training. The ultimate aim is to find flow. In his book *Flow*, Mihaly Csikszentmihalyi describes the peak state as one characterized by deep concentration, responsiveness, effectiveness, profound enjoyment, loss of sense of self, and an altered sense of time—the ideal conditions for success. RMD

Reframe Your Threats as Challenges

Whether you view something as a threat or a challenge is a matter of perspective and has very different effects on your physiology.

Threat

- ✗ Anxiety increases
- ✗ Blood pressure rises
- ✗ Air flow (VO$_2$max) decreases
- ✗ Energy (glucose) is depleted

Challenge

- ✓ Thinking is clear & focused
- ✓ Blood flow increases
- ✓ Oxygen intake improves
- ✓ Energy is produced

Head Games for Mental Toughness

Here are some strategies that foster confidence, keep you in the zone, and boost your performance.

❋ Power Poses

How you carry your body can impact hormonal production and cognitive functioning. Slouching can slow down brain chemistry, while standing tall and open can increase testosterone and cortisol levels, priming the body for maximum output. Next time you're on the start line, think about emulating Wonder Woman!

❋ Mantras & Power Words

Repeating positive statements during exercise is proven to improve performance by reducing activity in the fear center of the brain. *Joy*, *fast*, *fit*, and *presence* are some of the words Ro wrote on her hand prior to big races. These words helped center her in the final moments before the gun and served as a reminder of why she runs.

❋ Clothing as Costume

There is power in clothing. Studies have shown that what you wear can affect your performance on cognitive exams. Before your next race, pick a race kit that makes you feel like a badass.

❋ Mood Shifters

When killing time before a race, have on hand some of the things that put you in a good mood—a book, show, movie, playlist, photos, lucky clothes, gratitude list, or quotes. A few of your favorite things will buffer the stress and help keep you in a relaxed state until game time. Reading humorous books has saved Ro from burning too much nervous energy while waiting for races.

Warning: Avoid the energy zappers—people who make you feel worse after hanging with them. Be mindful of your energy, and protect it!

joy free fast fun

✳ Visual Cues

Symbols or graphics are interpreted by the brain almost instantaneously, triggering positive emotions and keeping you relaxed during competition. Lauren visualizes a lion in the final laps of a 5K because it prompts her to be ferocious and courageous in that crucial last 400 meters. A simple smiley face can remind you to have fun.

✳ Relaxation Techniques

Did you know that you can train your body to completely relax at the sound of a word? Practice relaxation techniques before races and workouts, during hectic travel, and before going to bed. For those athletes who find it hard to control their excitement before races, mindful

belly breathing will bring their awareness into their body.

✳ What-Ifs

Heading into a race, you want to be aware of the different scenarios you could face. Have a plan for what you will do if the race goes out fast, if it goes out slow, if you find yourself up front, if it's really windy, and so forth. Playing out the scenarios in your mind will save you crucial energy in the heat of the battle. Use the Race-Day Plans, pp. 212–17, to help you plan for some of the what-ifs.

✳ Visualization

Studying races or visualizing yourself running the race is an effective strategy for improving your form, your technique, or your tactics. This activates mirror neurons and instills in your brain what you are trying to do. Imagine how you'll feel at different points of the race, what sounds and sights you will observe, and so on. If you are running for someone or for a cause, then picture that when the going gets tough.

Mental toughness is an athlete's ability to be consistent and have self-control in training and competition.

The Mind's Role in Performance

UNDER-PERFORMANCE

- Needy
- Anxious + distracted
- Unworthy + unprepared
- Self-conscious
- Focused on outcome
- Threatened
- Unrealistic
- Rigid

BEST PERFORMANCE

- Mastery + practice
- Present
- Enthusiastic
- Focused + attentive
- Focused on process
- Challenged
- Realistic
- Open

No matter what level we compete at, we all want to get more out of ourselves. Mind-set can make the difference. Before your next race, do a check-in to see how you can shift your state of mind for your best performance.

RACE-DAY PLAN

RACE   1500m final

DATE   3/7

TIME   530 pm

LOCATION   Turin, Italy

NOTES ON EVENT & COURSE

weird starter
gun sound

GOALS

1. get in good position

2. be patient + in control
   4-5 laps

3. take chance when it comes!
   not easy - bring it on :)

SCHEDULE

START TIME	530 :)	on fire! Bliss
GO TO LINE	520	feel good :)
STRETCH	500	
WARM-UP	430	
CHECK-IN	400	

SCENARIOS

A. Top girls go out fast
   - settle in top 5-7
   - be ready for last 4 laps

B. They go out slow
   - watch footing + be
   ready for burn up!

C.

LOGISTICS

RELAX   330 - 430 read journal
         listen to tunes

EAT   400 coffee pb & j

TRAVEL   dep hotel @ 300

MY MANTRA

LOVE it ♡
RELAX :)
every lap, every step
patient - allow it unfold

To fill out your own Race-Day Plan go to page 212.

THIS WEEK'S FOCUS

Something you love about racing:

....

....

....

DATE	WORKOUT	MILEAGE / RATING
MON		
TUES		
WED		
THURS		

"When you put yourself on the line in a race and expose yourself to the unknown, you learn things about yourself that are very exciting."   Doris Brown Heritage, women's running pioneer

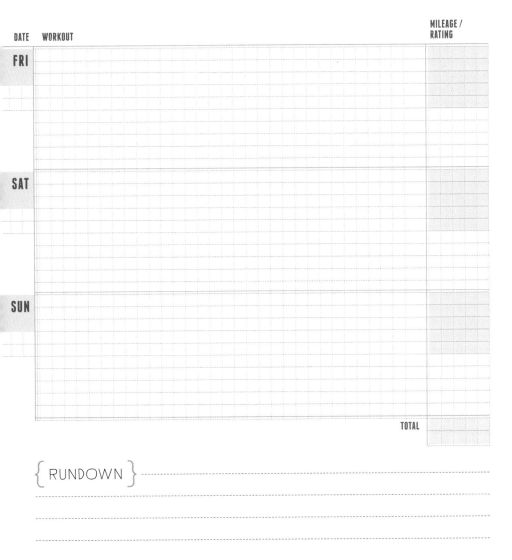

DATE	WORKOUT	MILEAGE / RATING
FRI		
SAT		
SUN		
	TOTAL	

{ RUNDOWN }

Negative things you tell yourself:

....

....

....

DATE	WORKOUT		MILEAGE / RATING
MON			
TUES			
WED			
THURS			

"Fear is gradually replaced by excitement and a simple desire to see what you can do on the day."

LAUREN FLESHMAN

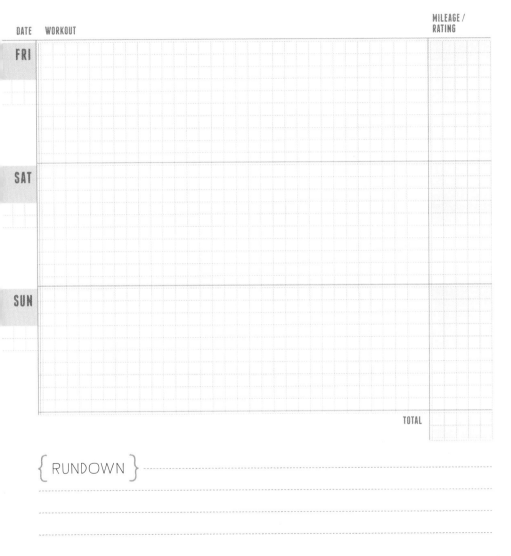

DATE	WORKOUT	MILEAGE / RATING
FRI		
SAT		
SUN		
	TOTAL	

{ RUNDOWN }

THIS WEEK'S FOCUS

You get into your zone by . . .

_____

_____

_____

DATE	WORKOUT	MILEAGE / RATING
MON		
TUES		
WED		
THURS		

"Be confident in the work you did to prepare for the race. Take a look back at your training logs to remind yourself that you've done everything possible to prepare. The race is the fun part, where you get to see the hard work pay off. Enjoy it." DESIREE LINDEN, OLYMPIAN & PRO MARATHONER

DATE	WORKOUT	MILEAGE / RATING
FRI		
SAT		
SUN		
	TOTAL	

{ RUNDOWN }

When you feel nervous, you stop and tell yourself...

DATE	WORKOUT	MILEAGE / RATING
MON		
TUES		
WED		
THURS		

"I'm always nervous. If I wasn't nervous, it would be weird. I get the same feeling at all the big races. It's part of the routine, and I accept it. It means I'm there and I'm ready."
ALLYSON FELIX, OLYMPIC GOLD & SILVER MEDALIST

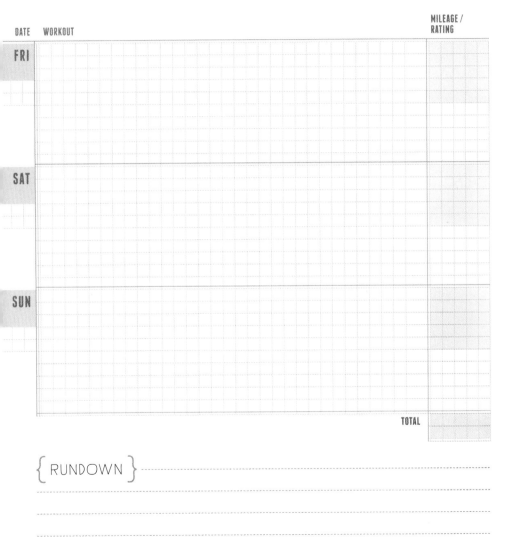

DATE	WORKOUT	MILEAGE / RATING
FRI		
SAT		
SUN		
	TOTAL	

{ RUNDOWN }

THIS WEEK'S FOCUS

The following will not change, no matter how you race:

....

....

....

DATE	WORKOUT	MILEAGE / RATING
MON		
TUES		
WED		
THURS		

"Competing in running gives me the confidence to just be myself in every other life setting."
DR. SARAH LESKO, FAMILY PHYSICIAN & MOTHER OF THREE BOYS

DATE	WORKOUT	MILEAGE / RATING
FRI		
SAT		
SUN		
	TOTAL	

{ RUNDOWN }

BELIEVE IN OBSTACLES AS OPPORTUNITIES

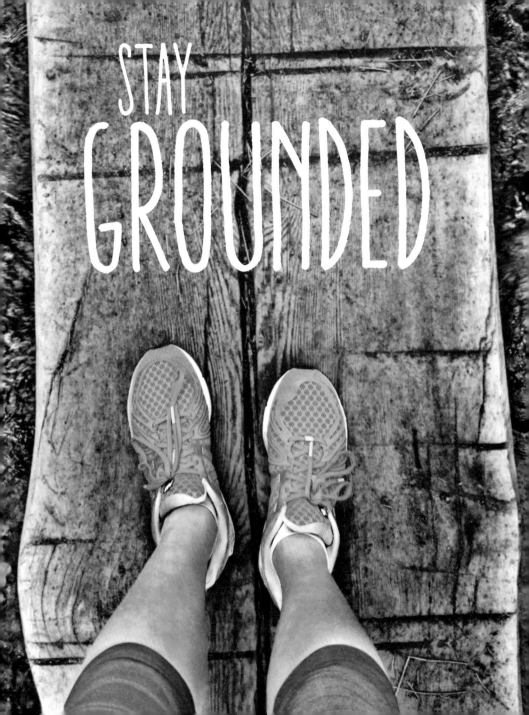

DEALING WITH ADVERSITY

Lauren

Nobody wants things to go wrong. Nobody plans to get bronchitis for three weeks during winter training, or to spend six weeks in a boot with a stress fracture. Nobody stays up nights wishing, *I'd really like to get my period the morning of the race*, or *I'd love to hit a performance plateau, or If only I could guarantee I'll hit this wall in this marathon.*

Every one of these things has happened to me, and I never once planned for it. Accumulating knowledge and experience helped me avoid or minimize some setbacks, but no one can prevent setbacks altogether. For example, learning the power of sleep and nutrition reduced my frequency of injury and illness. And yet, I still get injured or sick now and then.

One of the most empowering things about being a runner is realizing that you play a huge role in your own destiny. Hard work and dedication pay off. Good nutrition pays off. Developing mental strategies pays off. Competing with guts pays off. But this can feed the illusion that perfect preparation is possible and that achieving your goals is simply a matter of will.

As a rookie pro athlete, I sincerely believed that the entire point of setting goals was to one day achieve them. All my motivation and satisfaction were tied up in an attachment to the end game. From that viewpoint, setbacks were devastating, and I was riding an emotional roller coaster. It was a stressful, ineffective way to live.

The experiences I had and people I met changed my perspective. I began to realize that while taking responsibility for the things you *can* control is important, the unexpected will still happen, and when it does, the only thing you can control is how you react.

First, it's important to acknowledge disappointment before trying to hero up. Ironically, allowing yourself to feel bummed out can help you get over it faster. Just be aware that choosing to dwell in misery for too long makes you blind to the fact that obstacles are really opportunities in disguise. Be open to the lessons or experiences that may arise as a result of this "diversion." Consider that it may even be necessary for you to go through this challenge in order to reach your ultimate potential. Anyone who has achieved anything notable has been through significant obstacles on their way there. One could argue that periods of difficulty are actually a *requirement* to achieve greatness.

Another thing to consider is that the main reason for setting goals isn't to achieve them. It's like plugging a destination into a navigation system; it helps you identify a trajectory for moving through the world. Your goal puts you on a path to interact with certain types of people and to set up your life in a certain kind of way. My 15-year-old goal of being an Olympian has not been achieved yet, despite several close calls, but I certainly am no worse off for chasing it. Putting myself on that path has led to breakthrough performances, national championships, world travels, and incredible relationships. It has also put me through difficult experiences that have forced me to grow in ways I may not have

otherwise sought out. Setting that goal navigated me to my husband, served as my muse for writing, and put me in a position to write this page so I could reach out to you.

Make a goal, but loosen your death grip on it. Doing so does not make you any less likely to achieve it. With a journey-driven approach, you'll find more peace in the process and more clarity when stuff goes wrong, and you'll experience more life along the way. And when you do eventually achieve that goal, you'll feel much more fulfilled and ready to tackle the next one. 🔳

ATHLETIC PROGRESS

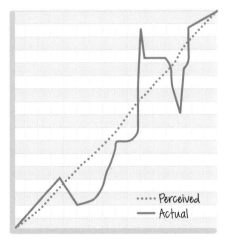

····· Perceived
—— Actual

How to Come Out Stronger on the Other End of a Setback

✳ Find a distraction

Take this time to experience the parts of your identity that running generally gets in the way of. Do yoga with your mom. Invest in relationships. Dive deeper into work or an extracurricular activity. Volunteer.

✳ Lower your stress

Stress slows the rate of healing, prolonging your misery. Look into ways to feel peaceful and spiritually fulfilled, starting with accepting your circumstances. Acceptance changes the energy around the setback, and it allows you to think logically about the next steps to take.

✳ See a physical therapist (PT)

Discover the root cause of the injury rather than just addressing the symptoms. A PT will be able to identify your areas of weakness so you can work on them.

✳ Do the little things

When you're healthy, it's easy to neglect gym work, strengthening exercises, and rehab. Injuries are a great opportunity to get back to basics and focus on core strength, Pilates, yoga, and foot exercises to create a strong foundation for your return to running, and doing so will make you more resilient and powerful in your next training cycle.

✳ Focus on what you can do

Crosstraining provides a great deal of crossover fitness, physically and mentally. Our favorite methods are ElliptiGO, swimming, water running, and elliptical training.

✳ Don't be afraid to do nothing

There will be days when you just can't motivate yourself to crosstrain, rehab, or do anything else. On days like this, rest is best. Even if you did nothing for months, you can return to peak fitness eventually. It might take longer, but that's okay. Your sanity and life enjoyment are more important than a couple weeks of missed training here or there.

Practice GRATITUDE

THINGS	OPPORTUNITIES	PEOPLE
I AM GRATEFUL FOR	I AM GRATEFUL FOR	I AM GRATEFUL FOR

While injuries and setbacks are infuriating and make you feel like a victim, one of the cures is cultivating gratitude.

"Be thankful for what you have; you'll end up having more. If you concentrate on what you don't have, you will never, ever have enough."
OPRAH WINFREY

THIS WEEK'S FOCUS

What's the worst-case scenario?

DATE	WORKOUT	MILEAGE / RATING
MON		
TUES		
WED		
THURS		

"When you recognize that failing doesn't make you a failure, you give yourself permission to try all sorts of things."

LAUREN FLESHMAN

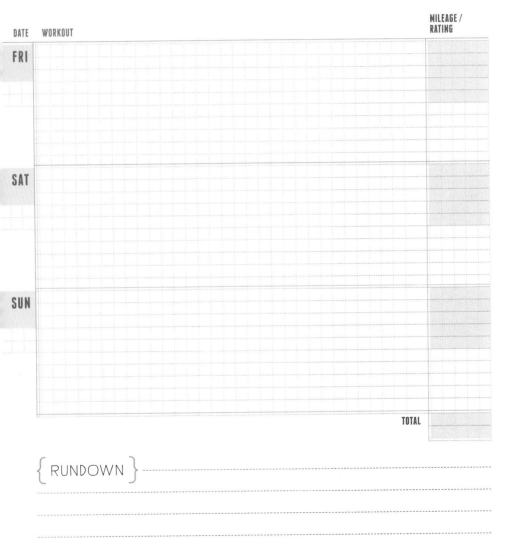

DATE	WORKOUT	MILEAGE / RATING
FRI		
SAT		
SUN		
	TOTAL	

{ RUNDOWN }

THIS WEEK'S FOCUS

The first step in picking yourself up is . . .

_____

_____

_____

DATE	WORKOUT	MILEAGE / RATING
MON		
TUES		
WED		
THURS		

"Acknowledge all of your small victories. They will add up to something great."

KARA GOUCHER, WORLD CHAMPIONSHIPS BRONZE MEDALIST

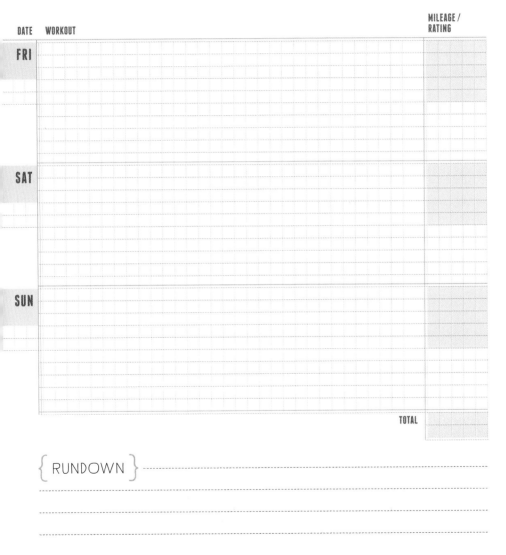

DATE	WORKOUT	MILEAGE / RATING
FRI		
SAT		
SUN		
	TOTAL	

{ RUNDOWN }

When things go wrong, you best process it by ...

DATE	WORKOUT	MILEAGE / RATING
MON		
TUES		
WED		
THURS		

"I've always been good at putting things behind me—I fall apart, do my crying bit, and then put it away and move on."

PAULA RADCLIFFE, MARATHON OLYMPIAN, WORLD CHAMPION & WORLD-RECORD HOLDER

DATE	WORKOUT	MILEAGE / RATING
FRI		
SAT		
SUN		
	TOTAL	

{ RUNDOWN }

THIS WEEK'S FOCUS

A setback that turned positive:

DATE	WORKOUT	MILEAGE / RATING
MON		
TUES		
WED		
THURS		

"Every time I fail I assume I will be a stronger person for it."

JOAN BENOIT SAMUELSON, FIRST WOMEN'S OLYMPIC MARATHON CHAMPION

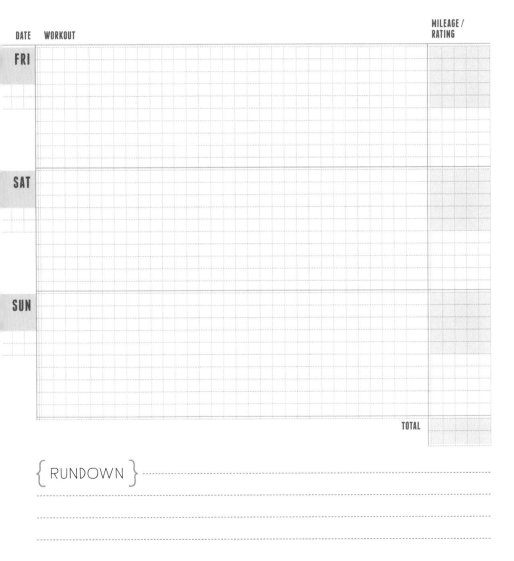

DATE	WORKOUT	MILEAGE / RATING
FRI		
SAT		
SUN		
	TOTAL	

{ RUNDOWN }

THIS WEEK'S FOCUS

A hard lesson you don't want to have to learn again:

_____

_____

_____

DATE	WORKOUT	MILEAGE / RATING
MON		
TUES		
WED		
THURS		

"In college I had three stress fractures in 18 months. The third one broke my spirit and I faced the idea of quitting the sport. This led me to recognize my love for the sport and competing. I will run regardless of whether I am at my former level."

MOLLY HUDDLE, USA CHAMPION & AMERICAN-RECORD HOLDER

DATE	WORKOUT	MILEAGE / RATING
FRI		
SAT		
SUN		
	TOTAL	

{ RUNDOWN }

CHECK-IN HOW I'M DOING . . .

THINK LIKE A PRO

Regardless of whether you are fast or slow, experienced or new to the sport, you will benefit from taking an honest look at the characteristics that hinder your progress and enjoyment. In his book *Turning Pro*, Steven Pressfield contrasts the mentality of an "amateur" and a "professional" writer, but his principles are applicable to athletes, too. Let's identify the kind of traits that will raise your game.

Be Courageous

A pro has the courage to listen to her heart and pursue her dreams regardless of what others think. She doesn't wait for her friends to get onboard. She makes her own way and helps others do the same. Amateurs, on the other hand, need external validation and can be afraid to show their true colors, being wary of criticism or rejection. This fear and uncertainty will prevent you from doing what you really want (and need) to do to follow your dreams.

Be Realistic

A pro knows from experience what is realistic and possible for her; therefore, she's not overly ambitious with her time, energy, and goals. This sensibility sets her up to be successful in her current position. Amateurs, on the other hand, often have unrealistic expectations that yield stress, chaos, and failure. They can be overly reliant on enthusiasm, which ebbs and flows. Enthusiasm is awesome, but if it morphs into overzealous ambition or fosters obsessive and unhealthy behavior, you might find yourself chasing unrealistic goals. Finding a good coach who can keep you grounded is a great help.

Be Resilient

The hardest thing about becoming a professional (athlete, artist, writer, you name it) is dealing with hard knocks, failures, and underperformances. The best pros accept these setbacks and recognize them as a form of validation within the competition arena. Amateurs are more likely to be defeated by failure or to overcompensate, which costs more in the long run. Failing simply means you are learning. Get knocked down. Stand up. Brush it off. After all, no one said it was going to be easy. Cultivate resilience from failure.

Do the Work

The professional knows that ultimately success (aka the outcome) is out of her control. She focuses instead on that which she can directly control—improving her technique, showing up for workouts, and recovering properly. The amateur is fixated on the goal. Her identity and value are on the line, raising the stakes. You cannot control the outcome, only your efforts to get there.

Be in It for the Long Haul

The most successful athletes train wisely and don't aim to outdo themselves every day. Pros conserve energy and enthusiasm to ensure longevity. They are the tortoise, not the hare. Long before they were pros, they put together weeks, months, and years of solid, consistent training. Many amateur athletes believe they need to "train like the pros" by doing a great deal of high-intensity work, but this is not physically or mentally sustainable. Seeking immediate, unrealistic improvements often leads to overtraining and injuries. Be confident in your ability and your plan. Shift your focus to appropriate training, and commit to the process.

Pocket the Payoff

Professionals are paid to train and compete, whereas most amateurs pay a significant cost to compete. However, there's another form of payment available to pros, amateurs, and everyone in between: the soul-sustaining, intrinsic rewards that come from pursuing excellence. Any pro will tell you that achieving a personal record is one of the most enjoyable and satisfying thrills experienced in sport. The feeling of progress is exhilarating. Personal growth, self-satisfaction, and mastery are priceless.

Anyone can adopt a professional state of mind—it's free, after all—but it's not easy. If you are frustrated with your results despite your best efforts, take some time to cultivate the traits that will help you tap into your full potential. ▯▮▯

State of mind QUIZ

PRO		AMATEUR
You build your life around the pursuit of your goals.	**PRIORITIES** 1 2 3 4 5	Your priorities are in constant conflict.
No excuses; you show up.	**CONSISTENCY** 1 2 3 4 5	You have good (and bad) excuses for not doing the work.
You are committed for the long term.	**COMMITMENT** 1 2 3 4 5	You are counting down to the next race and looking for the next great thing.
You take major blows and keep going.	**RESILIENCE** 1 2 3 4 5	You are defeated by setbacks.
You look for small, steady improvements.	**PRAGMATISM** 1 2 3 4 5	You are overambitious and never satisfied.
You are open to criticism, often using it to become better.	**ADAPTABILITY** 1 2 3 4 5	You take criticism or conflicting opinions personally.
You have a strong sense of who you are and where you are headed.	**CONFIDENCE** 1 2 3 4 5	You are constantly seeking validation and approval.
You vent and move on.	**EMOTIONAL WELL-BEING** 1 2 3 4 5	You ride a rollercoaster of ups and downs.
You focus on doing the work, enjoying the process.	**FOCUS** 1 2 3 4 5	You focus on the outcome above all else.
Resistance is your number-one foe, and you face it every day.	**RESOLVE** 1 2 3 4 5	You are out to beat Resistance.
You are dedicated to learning what works; mastery.	**TECHNIQUE** 1 2 3 4 5	You tend to work hard rather than work on technique.

New HABITS

Create some new habits that will truly honor your passion. Think about the changes you can make to be more professional in your approach to the sport.

I will keep my priorities straight. I will consistently show up. I will be committed for the long haul. I will be resilient. I will be realistic about my progress. I will know when to adapt. I will be confident. I will balance my emotions. I will focus on what's important. I will hold my resolve in the face of Resistance. I will give technique its due.

THIS WEEK'S FOCUS

You've already won because . . .

....

....

....

DATE	WORKOUT	MILEAGE / RATING
MON		
TUES		
WED		
THURS		

"You have the right to work only, but not for the results of work."

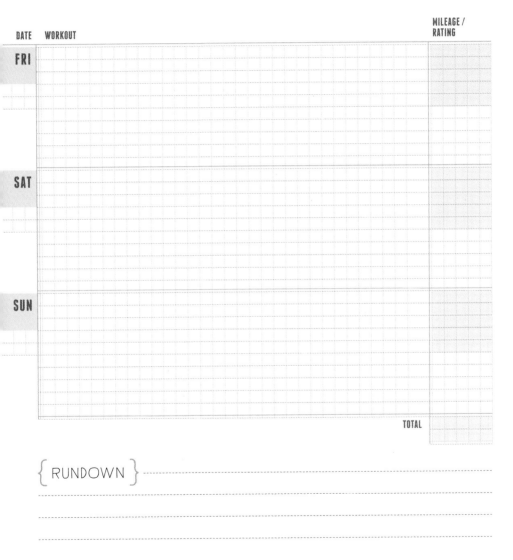

DATE	WORKOUT	MILEAGE / RATING
FRI		
SAT		
SUN		
	TOTAL	

{ RUNDOWN }

THIS WEEK'S FOCUS

The reason you will be successful:

_____

_____

_____

DATE	WORKOUT	MILEAGE / RATING
MON		
TUES		
WED		
THURS		

"Competition connects us to humanity, grounds us in humility, and gives us huevos—the courage to do big shit. These defining moments, big and small, make me more effective in work and life."
                                              SALLY BERGESEN, CEO & FOUNDER OF OISELLE

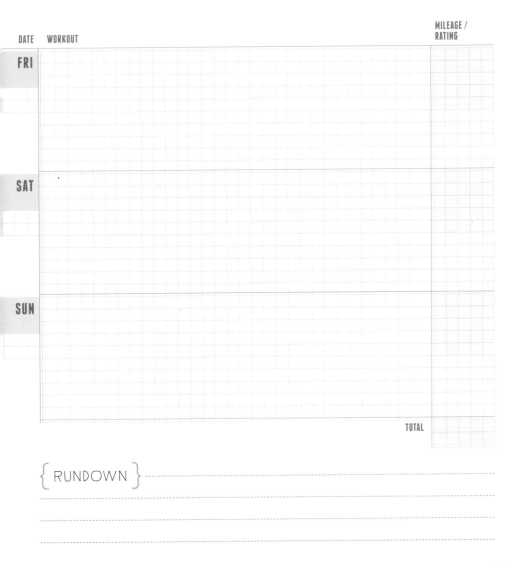

DATE	WORKOUT	MILEAGE / RATING
FRI		
SAT		
SUN		
	TOTAL	

{ RUNDOWN }

THIS WEEK'S FOCUS

The strongest parts of your preparation have been . . .

DATE	WORKOUT		MILEAGE / RATING
MON			
TUES			
WED			
THURS			

"Happiness is not a state to arrive at, but a manner of traveling."
                                    MARGARET LEE RUNBECK, AUTHOR

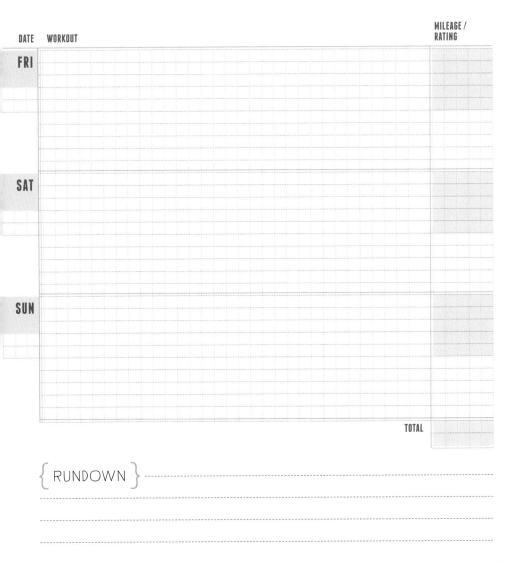

DATE	WORKOUT	MILEAGE / RATING
FRI		
SAT		
SUN		
		TOTAL

{ RUNDOWN }

THIS WEEK'S FOCUS

What is holding you back the most?

DATE	WORKOUT	MILEAGE / RATING
MON		
TUES		
WED		
THURS		

"For an athlete, the biggest pressure comes from within. You know what you want to do and what you're capable of."

PAULA RADCLIFFE, MARATHON OLYMPIAN, WORLD CHAMPION & WORLD-RECORD HOLDER

DATE	WORKOUT	MILEAGE / RATING
FRI		
SAT		
SUN		
	TOTAL	

{ RUNDOWN }

163

BELIEVE IN REST & REJUVENATION

RELAX & RECOVER

Lauren

Training makes us faster, right? Workouts make us stronger, tougher, and prepared for races. Well, kinda. If you don't prioritize recovery, all that hard work is for nothing, and instead of building you up, it will destroy you. Illness, injury, plateaus, underperformance . . . most of the frustrations running brings us come down to a lack of respect for proper recovery. Why is that?

The workouts are where the glitz and glamour are. The workouts are where we track our progress and where all the good battle stories are created. A 5-mile recovery jog frankly isn't that interesting, but physiology proves it's where the real magic happens.

Training hard doesn't build us up; it tears us down. Hard workouts create stress, break down muscle, tear up tissue, deplete nutrient stores, and leave us with fatigue. The body interprets all of this as a message that it needs to adapt, build more muscle, and make more red blood cells so it will be better prepared for the challenge next time. Our bodies are incredible in that way.

With time, stimulus, and proper recovery, our bodies will change to meet our demands, whether it's chopping wood or racing a marathon.

A hard workout is like wringing out a sponge. While you are squeezing it, it can't hold any liquid, but once you release your grip, it soaks everything in. If you only release your grip on the sponge halfway, you don't allow the sponge to absorb its full potential of water on the next go-around. A successful training plan is like squeezing and releasing a sponge over and over again. When you are younger and/or fitter, you can squeeze it more frequently. By experimenting and learning to listen to your body, you can find the right rhythm for you.

To successfully manage the stress in your life, it's important to realize that your training does not exist in a vacuum. Many people mistakenly separate their running life from their work, school, or relationships. The truth is, all stress takes water out of the same well, be it physical, mental, or emotional, and you only have one well to draw upon. Even after "good" stress such as a wedding or a family holiday, the body needs to repair itself. This is why it is crucial to do an honest audit of your lifestyle and your stress management strategies when pursuing athletic goals and figuring out how much recovery you need between workouts.

In order to recover, you need to get your body into a parasympathetic hormonal state. This is also known as the "rest and digest" state and is in direct opposition to the sympathetic "fight or flight" state. In the parasympathetic state you absorb nutrition and produce the hormones required to repair the body. Sleep is the single most important factor in recovering well; athletes who sleep eight hours at night are 87 percent less likely to get injured than athletes who sleep six hours! But it doesn't stop at sleep. When we are at peace, even if we are actively working, or managing projects, or driving in traffic, we put our body in a state that allows recovery. The vast majority of activities we do can be approached with or without excess stress. By bringing mindfulness to how we react to things, we can not only train and compete better but also be healthier and less susceptible to disease. **LF**

Dealing with
STRESS
(So You Can Recover)

We can't always control what happens around us, but we can control how we allow it to affect us. Physiologically speaking, all of these things have the potential to create an effect on our bodies that is equivalent to being chased by a lion.

1. On the next page, circle (and write in) things that have stressed you out in the past.

2. Cross off things that aren't worthy of depleting your well this year.

⋯⟩

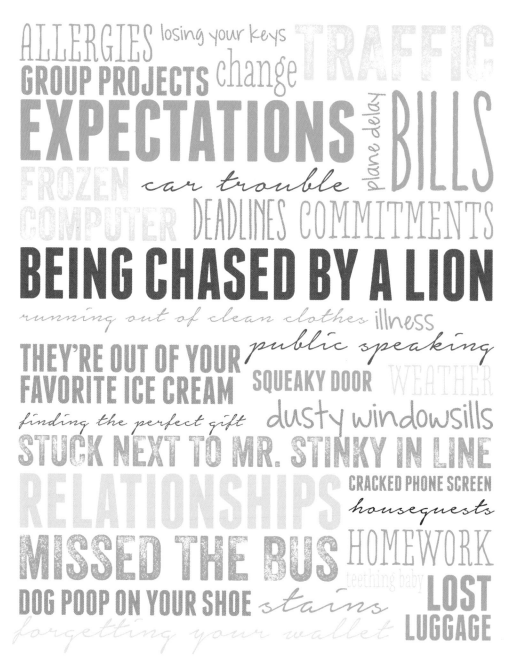

ALLERGIES losing your keys TRAFFIC
GROUP PROJECTS change
EXPECTATIONS BILLS
FROZEN car trouble plane delay
COMPUTER DEADLINES COMMITMENTS
BEING CHASED BY A LION
running out of clean clothes illness
THEY'RE OUT OF YOUR public speaking
FAVORITE ICE CREAM SQUEAKY DOOR WEATHER
finding the perfect gift dusty windowsills
STUCK NEXT TO MR. STINKY IN LINE
RELATIONSHIPS CRACKED PHONE SCREEN
houseguests
MISSED THE BUS HOMEWORK
teething baby
DOG POOP ON YOUR SHOE stains LOST
forgetting your wallet LUGGAGE

Our Favorite Recovery Strategies

For better recovery from training

✩ Develop a prehab (preventative rehab) routine that can become habit, such as loosening up key muscles and joints that tend to give you trouble before going out the door.

✩ Eat 200–250 calories that contain carbohydrate and some protein immediately following exercise to replace glycogen stores. A 4-to-1 ratio of carbs to protein works well.

✩ Create a short series of mindful stretches or yoga for after workouts.

✩ Wearing compression socks during and/or after hard training is like a hug for your legs!

For better daily recovery

✩ Eat nutritious, balanced foods. Ditch the processed foods and added sugar, which reduce the hormones needed for recovery.

✩ Keep alcohol in moderation. Drinking more than 1.5 servings of alcohol reduces quality REM sleep and recovery.

✩ Never be caught without a water bottle. Add carbohydrate and electrolyte products to it when training a lot to aid in absorption.

✩ Lying on the floor and putting your legs up the wall for a few minutes does wonders for blood flow and relaxation!

For better sleep

✩ Create a healthy sleep environment and a bedtime routine to help you sleep more peacefully.

✩ Catch a nap when you can! The harder you train, the more important this becomes. But for people like me who struggle to nap, putting your legs up the wall for at least five minutes and clearing your mind is extremely restorative.

THIS WEEK'S FOCUS

How are you appreciating your unique calling and ability?

....

....

....

DATE	WORKOUT	MILEAGE / RATING
MON		
TUES		
WED		
THURS		

"Anyone can work hard. The best have the discipline to recover."

LAUREN FLESHMAN

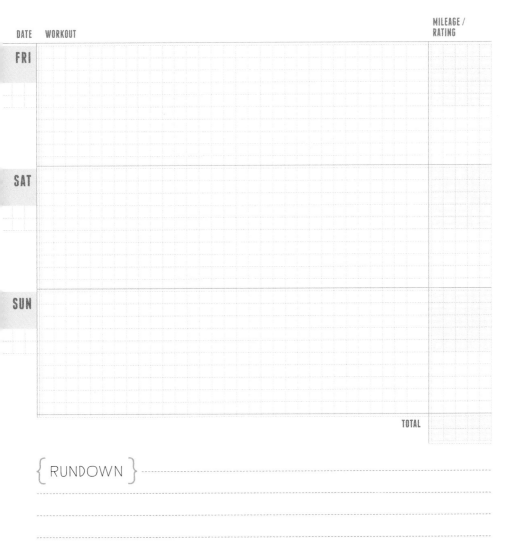

DATE	WORKOUT	MILEAGE / RATING
FRI		
SAT		
SUN		
	TOTAL	

{ RUNDOWN }

THIS WEEK'S FOCUS

You will improve your recovery by:

DATE	WORKOUT	MILEAGE / RATING
MON		
TUES		
WED		
THURS		

"My workout days are pretty intense, so I make sure to run very easy in between so I'm recovered enough to push hard on my workout days." KIM SMITH, THREE-TIME OLYMPIAN

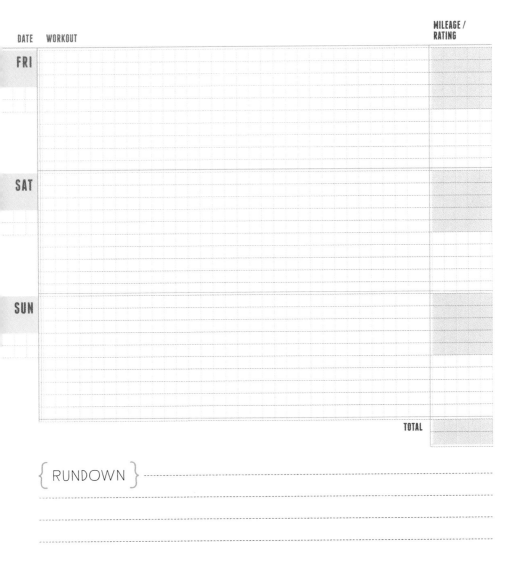

DATE	WORKOUT	MILEAGE / RATING
FRI		
SAT		
SUN		
	TOTAL	

{ RUNDOWN }

THIS WEEK'S FOCUS

You make restorative time by . . .

DATE	WORKOUT	MILEAGE / RATING
MON		
TUES		
WED		
THURS		

"Running is my meditation, mind flush, cosmic telephone, mood elevator, and spiritual communion."
LORRAINE MOLLER, OLYMPIC BRONZE MEDALIST

DATE	WORKOUT	MILEAGE / RATING
FRI		
SAT		
SUN		
	TOTAL	

{ RUNDOWN }

THIS WEEK'S FOCUS

Things you can move off your plate:

....

....

....

DATE	WORKOUT	MILEAGE / RATING
MON		
TUES		
WED		
THURS		

"Step with care and great tact and remember that Life's a Great Balancing Act."

DR. SEUSS, OH, THE PLACE YOU'LL GO!

DATE	WORKOUT	MILEAGE / RATING
FRI		
SAT		
SUN		
	TOTAL	

{ RUNDOWN }

Your ideal sleep habits:

- -

- -

- -

DATE	WORKOUT	MILEAGE / RATING
MON		
TUES		
WED		
THURS		

"Just like the exhale needs the inhale, our bodies need relaxation after exertion."
ROÍSÍN MCGETTIGAN-DUMAS

DATE	WORKOUT	MILEAGE / RATING
FRI		
SAT		
SUN		
	TOTAL	

{ RUNDOWN }

CHECK-IN HOW I'M DOING . . .

BELIEVE IN YOUR SUPPORT NETWORK

MOVING FROM ME TO US

Lauren

It's very rare for a person to self-motivate all the time. Everyone from newbies to pro athletes struggles with this. In my first eight years as a runner, I was surrounded by large teams with set schedules, and

while I enjoyed it, the prospect of independence in my running after graduation was exciting! I could run at 7 a.m. or 8 at night if I wanted to, at whatever pace I wanted to, and I had the freedom to move my workout schedule around based on how I was feeling on the day. What happened surprised me.

Quite often I found it excruciatingly difficult to get out the door, even though I was setting out to do something I supposedly loved. And without a group training schedule to adhere to, I spent a lot of time waffling on what I should or shouldn't do, and when. When I had a great workout, I felt satisfied, but my hand itched to high-five someone. And while I enjoyed more peace and quiet on my solitary runs, I found myself missing the story lines of my running buddies' lives. Ultimately, I realized that those group runs were life education and mentorship as much as chitchat. In the

10 years since, I've made it a priority to be a part of some kind of community in my running, whether it's daily runs with world-class athletes, weekly runs with a recreation group based out of a local running store, or engaging with the online communities that Picky Bars, Oiselle, and my blog facilitate.

I've learned that there are specific things that make a community helpful, and things that don't, and that when we willingly weave our time into one another's lives, something greater than the sum of its parts is created. The running communities I am a part of have changed my outlook on life, which then feeds back into my approach to running. Community is the balance point between the two, keeping me from teeter-tottering too far in any one direction.

You don't necessarily have to have a running community to have a fulfilling running experience, but it can add a lot of richness, depth, motivation, and inspiration. Or it can add stress, frustration, and distraction . . . the value is determined by the company you keep and the environment you all foster together.

In my travels, I visit a lot of running communities to speak and jump in for a run. For one day I am like a new ingredient tossed into their soup recipe. Sometimes I try to go in like a potato—neutral, not changing the flavor dynamics. Other times, when things need shaking up, I go in like a habanero. The most rewarding running communities are the ones where the members are aware of the flavor they each bring to the soup and where they work to enhance one another. They show up intending to both take energy from the group and give energy back.

Your running community can take many forms. It can be simply you and one running buddy, a club, a team, a charity, or an online community. There are examples of each of these that will amplify your running experience, and examples that will be destructive to it. The people you surround yourself with will weave into your life, your mentality, your perception of what's possible and what isn't. So choose your community wisely. If you find a good one, protect it and shape it. Watch out for negative things that can spoil it and reduce its value to the members' lives.

No matter where you stack up when it comes to speed or distance, stake claim to your group and run with pride. Your running will soar by being a part of something bigger than yourself. ▪

Do Your Part to Make a Great Running Community

What to Contribute

- ✓ Good energy
- ✓ Generosity
- ✓ Unique skills and experience
- ✓ Consistency
- ✓ Confidence boosts for others

What to Take Away

- ✓ Inspiration
- ✓ Structure
- ✓ Balance
- ✓ Accountability
- ✓ Knowledge
- ✓ Friendship

What to Watch Out For

- ✗ Gossip
- ✗ Disordered eating
- ✗ Judgment and intolerance
- ✗ Competition that goes too far (leave it on the racecourse)
- ✗ A zero-sum attitude toward success

How would you like to be remembered?

DATE	WORKOUT	MILEAGE / RATING
MON		
TUES		
WED		
THURS		

"And as we let our own light shine, we unconsciously give other people permission to do the same. As we are liberated from our own fear, our presence automatically liberates others."
MARIANNE WILLIAMSON, AUTHOR & LECTURER

DATE	WORKOUT	MILEAGE / RATING
FRI		
SAT		
SUN		
	TOTAL	

{ RUNDOWN }

THIS WEEK'S FOCUS

Who and what fill you most with love?

DATE	WORKOUT	MILEAGE / RATING
MON		
TUES		
WED		
THURS		

"The one training tool I couldn't live without is my training partners. It's so much easier to get out the door when you have someone to run with and push you on workout days."

KIM SMITH, THREE-TIME OLYMPIAN

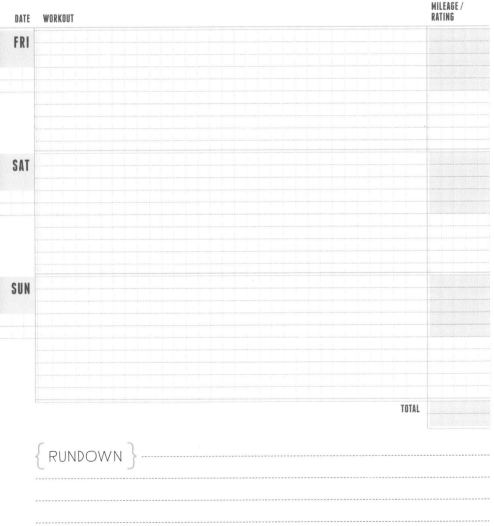

DATE	WORKOUT	MILEAGE / RATING
FRI		
SAT		
SUN		
	TOTAL	

{ RUNDOWN }

THIS WEEK'S FOCUS

Key people influenced by your approach to running:

DATE	WORKOUT	MILEAGE / RATING
MON		
TUES		
WED		
THURS		

"My sisters in sport help me transcend my own ability, and more importantly they make the process FUN."

ROÍSÍN MCGETTIGAN-DUMAS

DATE	WORKOUT	MILEAGE / RATING
FRI		
SAT		
SUN		
	TOTAL	

{ RUNDOWN }

Who brings out the best in you? The worst?

....

....

....

DATE	WORKOUT	MILEAGE / RATING
MON		
TUES		
WED		
THURS		

"Who you hang out with determines what you dream about and what you collide with. And the collisions and the dreams lead to your changes. And the changes are what you become. Change the outcome by changing your circle." SETH GODIN, *AUTHOR & ENTREPRENEUR*

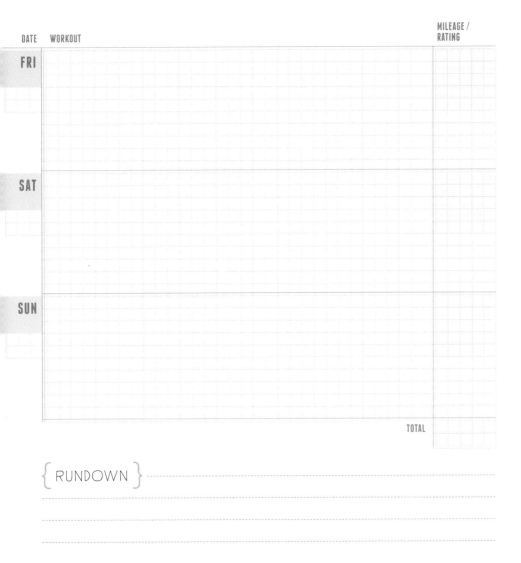

DATE	WORKOUT	MILEAGE / RATING
FRI		
SAT		
SUN		
	TOTAL	

{ RUNDOWN }

Qualities you bring to your community:

_____

_____

_____

DATE	WORKOUT	MILEAGE / RATING
MON		
TUES		
WED		
THURS		

"My coach has often saved me from getting in my own way by bringing an outside and less emotional view of my situation." MOLLY HUDDLE, USA CHAMPION & AMERICAN-RECORD HOLDER

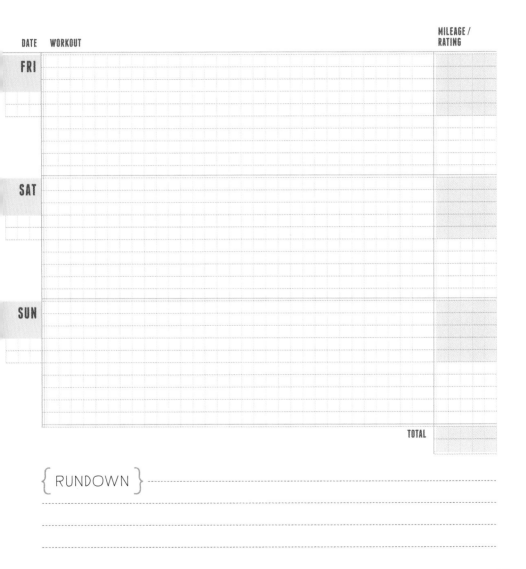

DATE	WORKOUT	MILEAGE / RATING
FRI		
SAT		
SUN		
	TOTAL	

{ RUNDOWN }

CHECK-IN HOW I'M DOING . . .

BELIEVE IN YOUR JOURNEY

LOOKING BACK TO MOVE FORWARD

By taking the time to reflect, we can create stepping-stones to bigger, better accomplishments. Throughout my career as a pro runner, my coach and I sat down at the end of every year to review the season. I often found myself wanting more from any given season, but my coach insisted we focus on setting an optimistic mind-set for the months of

arduous training that lay ahead. We looked back at my race results to identify what we did right and what we would've changed. We identified my weaknesses, usually tempo runs and longer workouts, and made a plan to work on them. My coach was adamant that we continue to develop my strengths, too. For me, these were my speed and technical ability. I walked away from those meetings buzzing, ready for action and armed with a clear vision and a plan of attack!

If you've been using your journal regularly, by now you have a collection of data that you can use to analyze and identify patterns, see what worked and what didn't, and determine what to repeat and what to change. You'll be

able to determine how much mileage is too much, or too little. It will become clear which workouts worked best before races. With these insights, you can take action to improve and progress as an athlete. Your journal can empower your decision making in the year ahead.

Whether it was good or bad, the past season can fuel your fire. Disappointment often acts as a catalyst for change and improvement. Conversely, if things went well, you now have a blueprint for how to re-create success and cut down on the guesswork. The worksheets that follow will help you take this new knowledge and act on it. (Warriors, you'll be tempted to skip this section . . . Don't. You don't want to keep repeating the same mistakes!) RMD

REFLECT on your season

SUCCESSES	DISAPPOINTMENTS

Ask yourself... What or who made it happen—you, your support system, your environment? What did you learn?

TROUBLESHOOT your goal-setting

GOAL

- ☐ This goal was realistic.
- ☐ I remained focused on the process, not the result.
- ☐ I made this goal a priority, giving it my best effort.
- ☐ This goal is still meaningful to me.

  What's next?

GOAL

- ☐ This goal was realistic.
- ☐ I remained focused on the process, not the result.
- ☐ I made this goal a priority, giving it my best effort.
- ☐ This goal is still meaningful to me.

  What's next?

GOAL

- ☐ This goal was realistic.
- ☐ I remained focused on the process, not the result.
- ☐ I made this goal a priority, giving it my best effort.
- ☐ This goal is still meaningful to me.

  What's next?

Did you hit your target this season? Revisit your goals (pp. 24–27) using this worksheet to identify what might have tripped you up.

GOAL

☐ This goal was realistic.
☐ I remained focused on the process, not the result.
☐ I made this goal a priority, giving it my best effort.
☐ This goal is still meaningful to me.
What's next?

GOAL

☐ This goal was realistic.
☐ I remained focused on the process, not the result.
☐ I made this goal a priority, giving it my best effort.
☐ This goal is still meaningful to me.
What's next?

GOAL

☐ This goal was realistic.
☐ I remained focused on the process, not the result.
☐ I made this goal a priority, giving it my best effort.
☐ This goal is still meaningful to me.
What's next?

THIS WEEK'S FOCUS

What did you do well this year?

_____

_____

_____

DATE	WORKOUT	MILEAGE / RATING
MON		
TUES		
WED		
THURS		

"Running has taught me to love my brain, my body, and what both can do for me when I use them wisely and appreciate them." — RESIDENT PHYSICIAN MEGGIE SMITH

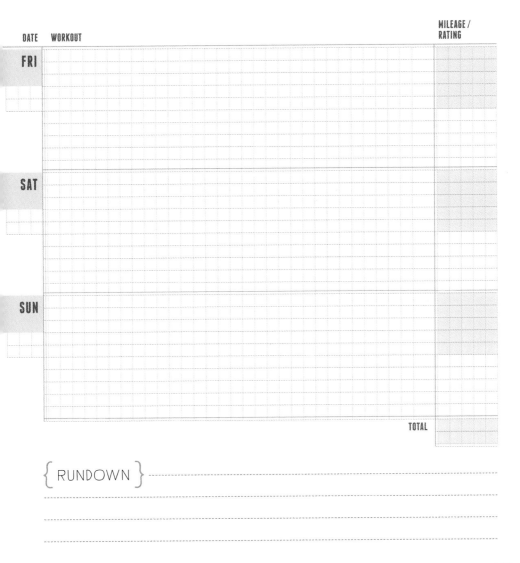

DATE	WORKOUT	MILEAGE / RATING
FRI		
SAT		
SUN		
		TOTAL

{ RUNDOWN }

What would you do differently next year?

....

....

....

DATE	WORKOUT	MILEAGE / RATING
MON		
TUES		
WED		
THURS		

"You either win, or you learn."
    J. J. CLARKE, LONGTIME COACH AT THE UNIVERSITY OF TENNESSEE

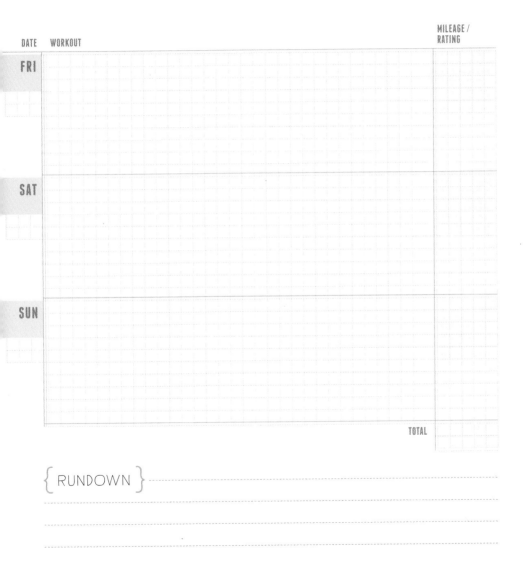

DATE	WORKOUT	MILEAGE / RATING
FRI		
SAT		
SUN		
	TOTAL	

{ RUNDOWN }

THIS WEEK'S FOCUS

What was the best part?

DATE	WORKOUT	MILEAGE / RATING
MON		
TUES		
WED		
THURS		

"Your greatest runs are rarely measured by racing success. They are moments in time when running allows you to see how wonderful your life is."

KARA GOUCHER, WORLD CHAMPIONSHIPS BRONZE MEDALIST

DATE	WORKOUT	MILEAGE / RATING
FRI		
SAT		
SUN		
	TOTAL	

{ RUNDOWN }

THIS WEEK'S FOCUS

What has been most surprising?

DATE	WORKOUT	MILEAGE / RATING
MON		
TUES		
WED		
THURS		

"There are victories of the soul and spirit. Sometimes, even if you lose, you win."
ELIE WIESEL, HOLOCAUST SURVIVOR & NOBEL PRIZE–WINNING AUTHOR

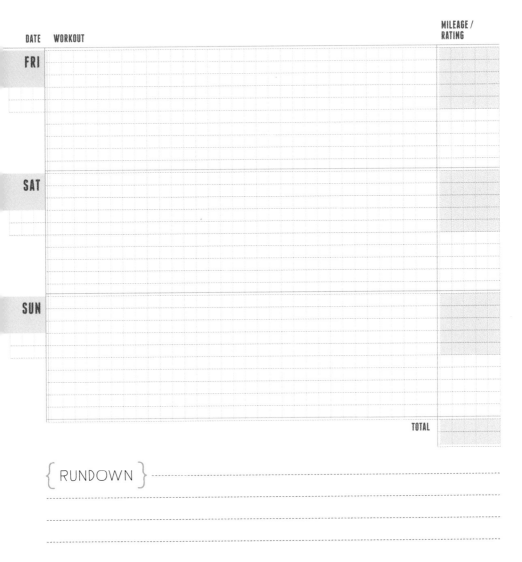

DATE	WORKOUT	MILEAGE / RATING
FRI		
SAT		
SUN		
	TOTAL	

{ RUNDOWN }

What lesson will you take with you into training?

....

....

....

DATE	WORKOUT	MILEAGE / RATING
MON		
TUES		
WED		
THURS		

"I let the space between where I am and where I need to be inspire me."
   ADRIANNE HASLET-DAVIS, BALLROOM DANCER, WRITER & BOSTON MARATHON BOMBINGS SURVIVOR

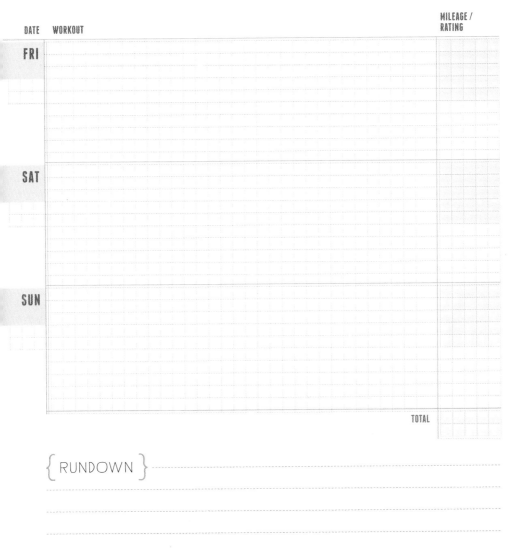

DATE	WORKOUT	MILEAGE / RATING
FRI		
SAT		
SUN		
	TOTAL	

{ RUNDOWN }

BELIEVE IN YOUR DREAMS

RACE-DAY PLANS

RACE	GOALS
	1.
DATE	
TIME	2.
LOCATION	
NOTES ON EVENT & COURSE	3.

SCHEDULE	SCENARIOS
START TIME	A.
GO TO LINE	
STRETCH	
WARM-UP	B.
CHECK-IN	

LOGISTICS	C.
RELAX	
	MY MANTRA
EAT	
TRAVEL	

RACE

DATE

TIME

LOCATION

NOTES ON EVENT & COURSE

GOALS

1.

2.

3.

SCHEDULE

START TIME

GO TO LINE

STRETCH

WARM-UP

CHECK-IN

SCENARIOS

A.

B.

LOGISTICS

RELAX

EAT

TRAVEL

C.

MY MANTRA

RACE-DAY PLANS

RACE

DATE

TIME

LOCATION

NOTES ON EVENT & COURSE

GOALS

1.

2.

3.

SCHEDULE

START TIME

GO TO LINE

STRETCH

WARM-UP

CHECK-IN

SCENARIOS

A.

B.

LOGISTICS

RELAX

EAT

TRAVEL

C.

MY MANTRA

RACE

DATE

TIME

LOCATION

NOTES ON EVENT & COURSE

GOALS

1.

2.

3.

SCHEDULE

START TIME

GO TO LINE

STRETCH

WARM-UP

CHECK-IN

SCENARIOS

A.

B.

LOGISTICS

RELAX

EAT

TRAVEL

C.

MY MANTRA

RACE-DAY PLANS

RACE	GOALS
	1.
DATE	
TIME	2.
LOCATION	
NOTES ON EVENT & COURSE	3.

SCHEDULE	SCENARIOS
START TIME	A.
GO TO LINE	
STRETCH	
WARM-UP	B.
CHECK-IN	

LOGISTICS	C.
RELAX	
	MY MANTRA
EAT	
TRAVEL	

RACE

DATE

TIME

LOCATION

NOTES ON EVENT & COURSE

SCHEDULE

START TIME

GO TO LINE

STRETCH

WARM-UP

CHECK-IN

LOGISTICS

RELAX

EAT

TRAVEL

GOALS

1.

2.

3.

SCENARIOS

A.

B.

C.

MY MANTRA

RACE REVIEWS

No single race, not even the Olympics, is the end-all, be-all. Every performance is simply a snapshot in the moving picture of your running life. Take time to review and learn from your races.

DATE	RACE	RESULT

WHAT I LEARNED

HOW I WAS BRILLIANT

WHAT I WOULD CHANGE

DATE	RACE	RESULT

WHAT I LEARNED

HOW I WAS BRILLIANT

WHAT I WOULD CHANGE

DATE	RACE	RESULT

WHAT I LEARNED

HOW I WAS BRILLIANT

WHAT I WOULD CHANGE

"Make the race your playground, not your proving ground."

LAUREN FLESHMAN

DATE	RACE	RESULT

WHAT I LEARNED

HOW I WAS BRILLIANT

WHAT I WOULD CHANGE

DATE	RACE	RESULT

WHAT I LEARNED

HOW I WAS BRILLIANT

WHAT I WOULD CHANGE

DATE	RACE	RESULT

WHAT I LEARNED

HOW I WAS BRILLIANT

WHAT I WOULD CHANGE

RACE REVIEWS

DATE	RACE	RESULT

WHAT I LEARNED

HOW I WAS BRILLIANT

WHAT I WOULD CHANGE

DATE	RACE	RESULT

WHAT I LEARNED

HOW I WAS BRILLIANT

WHAT I WOULD CHANGE

DATE	RACE	RESULT

WHAT I LEARNED

HOW I WAS BRILLIANT

WHAT I WOULD CHANGE

DATE	RACE		RESULT

WHAT I LEARNED

HOW I WAS BRILLIANT

WHAT I WOULD CHANGE

WHAT I LEARNED

HOW I WAS BRILLIANT

WHAT I WOULD CHANGE

WHAT I LEARNED

HOW I WAS BRILLIANT

WHAT I WOULD CHANGE

RACE CALENDAR { JAN–JUN }

Become a fan! Follow our favorite sport. You'll recognize many of our sisters in sport competing for wins!

	RACE	NOTES
JAN	**Houston Half-Marathon & 10K**	This fast, flat course was the home of the 2012 U.S. Olympic marathon trials and serves as the U.S.A. Half-Marathon Championships race.
	Polar Plunge	Cities around the world have special events to kick off the new year, many of which involve a symbolic plunge into an ice-cold body of water to wash oneself clean of the past year and start fresh.
FEB	**New Balance Indoor Grand Prix**	The pro indoor track circuit kicks into full swing at Boston's Reggie Lewis Center on a 200-meter indoor track in front of raving crowds.
	NYRR Millrose Games	This indoor track meet has been held for more than 100 years and continues to boast the premier mile races of the season.
	U.S.A. Cross-Country Championships	Cross country is a sport of mud and hills, where grit and toughness abound. This national championship doubles as a trial for the world championships held biannually.
	Tokyo Marathon	This is the first of six races in the World Marathon Majors. $1 million is given to the athlete with the greatest two-year overall series performance.
MAR	**NCAA Indoor Championships**	Top collegiate athletes and teams battle it out for NCAA track & field titles. Plenty of drama and breakthrough performances from rising stars.
	European Athletics Championships/ World Indoor Championships	In alternating years, the European Athletics or World Indoor Track Championships is held somewhere around the globe. Athletes race for national pride and medals.

	RACE	NOTES
APR	**Boston Marathon**	For avid runners, qualifying for Boston is like qualifiying for the Olympics—qualification times vary by age and sex. A 5K and road mile attract top elites and more runners who want in on the #BostonStrong environment.
	London Marathon	This World Marathon Majors event has become the largest donor to charities in the world thanks to the money raised by its participants. Paula Radcliffe's world record and Deena Kastor's American record were set here.
MAY	**Payton Jordan Invitational**	An evening distance carnival that almost always guarantees perfect conditions on Stanford's campus in California. This is the place for track athletes to hit fast times early in the season.
	IAAF World Relays	A new event to be contested once every four years, the top nations assemble relay teams ranging from 4 × 100m to the 4 × 1500m. Batons are dropped, collisions occur, and magic team chemistry gives you goosebumps.
	High school state meets	Kids across the nation begin to fight for state track & field titles and school pride while college coaches scout for recruits.
JUN	**Prefontaine Classic**	The world's best athletes compete at historic Hayward Field in Eugene, Oregon. This has been ranked as the number-one track meet in the world.
	Oakley New York Mini 10K	The first women-only road race in the world, NYRR's Mini boasts a stacked pro field leading 7,000-plus participants through Central Park.
	Flora Women's Mini Marathon	Home of the largest women-only race in the world, with more than 40,000 participants annually, this race deserves a shout-out!
	NCAA Track & Field Championships	It's been called the best meet in track & field for the March Madness–like intensity of collegiate athletes fighting for titles for their universities.

RACE CALENDAR { JUL–DEC }

	RACE	NOTES
JUL	European Circuit	All through the summer, track & field fills huge stadiums in Europe just as basketball does in the United States. Look up "Diamond League" to follow international stars chasing big prize purses and the series prize—a hefty diamond.
	AJC Peachtree Road Race	The largest men's and women's 10K in the world and site of the U.S.A. Road 10K Championships.
	Badwater 135 Ultramarathon	This race is recognized globally as the world's toughest, running over three mountain ranges and through the desert's scorching heat, putting human survival to the ultimate test.
AUG	IAAF World Championships OR Olympics	The focus of the year for pro athletes. Fast times don't matter—it's all about strategy and tactics. Each event has qualifying rounds, making it extremely difficult for athletes to make finals and win medals to bring back to their home countries.
	European/ Pan American Championships	Championship races are broken up geographically, providing a slightly smaller environment for athletes to contend for medals.
	Leadville Trail 100 Run	This ultramarathon reaches elevations as high as 12,600 feet as it crosses the Colorado Rockies and was the setting of international best seller *Born to Run*, a book that popularized the minimalist shoe trend.
SEP	U.S.A. 5K Road Championships	Home of Ro and elites Kim Smith, Molly Huddle, and Amy Hastings. Race in downtown Providence, Rhode Island, in the best conditions of the year.
	NYRR Fifth Avenue Mile	A 1-mile stretch of Fifth Avenue in New York City is closed to traffic for elites and recreational athletes to take a crack at a mile PR.
	Berlin Marathon	Known for blazing-fast times and record setters, this destination marathon is another World Marathon Majors stop.
	Ironman 70.3 World Championship	Athletes compete in a half-marathon after swimming 1.2 miles and biking 56 miles. The top pros finish in about 4 hours, and there is a very strong age-group culture.

	RACE	NOTES
OCT	**Chicago Marathon**	The World Marathon Majors moves to the Windy City for another serving of extraordinary endurance and pace. On a good-weather day, this is a less grueling course than New York City or Boston and serves up fast times.
	Ironman World Championship	In Kona every year, the best age groupers and pros in the world compete in a marathon in blazing heat and humidity alongside lava flows after swimming 2.4 miles and biking 112 miles. The top women run the marathon in under 3 hours.
NOV	**NYC Marathon**	The Big Apple hosts the World Marathon Majors and the largest marathon in the world, with international runners making up half the field.
	NCAA Cross Country Nationals	The Big Dance is where the best collegiate teams and individuals battle for the national crown. Always epic.
	Turkey Trot	The best way to earn your Thanksgiving feast in advance, all around the country.
DEC	**Footlocker Cross Country Championships**	This famous national high school meet brings together the cream of the crop of U.S. high school athletes competing as individuals.
	USATF National Club Cross Country Championships	The team championships for running clubs across the nation, from masters to the pro level. A unique chance for pros and amateurs from the same club to run as teammates.

BELIEVE IN THE UNKNOWN

CHANGE GEARS

PACE CHART

This pace chart was developed with training in mind. If you want to run 800-meter intervals at your 5K goal pace, locate your goal pace in the 5K column and follow it straight over to the 800 meters column. For example, if your 5K goal time is 20:00, your 800m interval goal pace is 3:12.

200m	400m	800m	1200m	1600m	5K	10K	13.1 mi.	26.2 mi.
0:00:30	0:01:00	0:02:00	0:03:00	0:04:00	0:12:30	0:25:00	0:52:45	1:45:29
0:00:31	0:01:01	0:02:02	0:03:03	0:04:04	0:12:43	0:25:25	0:53:37	1:47:15
0:00:31	0:01:02	0:02:04	0:03:06	0:04:08	0:12:55	0:25:50	0:54:30	1:49:00
0:00:32	0:01:03	0:02:06	0:03:09	0:04:12	0:13:08	0:26:15	0:55:23	1:50:46
0:00:32	0:01:04	0:02:08	0:03:12	0:04:16	0:13:20	0:26:40	0:56:16	1:52:31
0:00:33	0:01:05	0:02:10	0:03:15	0:04:20	0:13:33	0:27:05	0:57:08	1:54:17
0:00:33	0:01:06	0:02:12	0:03:18	0:04:24	0:13:45	0:27:30	0:58:01	1:56:02
0:00:34	0:01:07	0:02:14	0:03:21	0:04:28	0:13:58	0:27:55	0:58:54	1:57:48
0:00:34	0:01:08	0:02:16	0:03:24	0:04:32	0:14:10	0:28:20	0:59:46	1:59:33
0:00:35	0:01:09	0:02:18	0:03:27	0:04:36	0:14:23	0:28:45	1:00:39	2:01:19
0:00:35	0:01:10	0:02:20	0:03:30	0:04:40	0:14:35	0:29:10	1:01:32	2:03:04
0:00:36	0:01:11	0:02:22	0:03:33	0:04:44	0:14:48	0:29:35	1:02:25	2:04:50
0:00:36	0:01:12	0:02:24	0:03:36	0:04:48	0:15:00	0:30:00	1:03:17	2:06:35
0:00:37	0:01:13	0:02:26	0:03:39	0:04:52	0:15:13	0:30:25	1:04:10	2:08:21
0:00:37	0:01:14	0:02:28	0:03:42	0:04:56	0:15:25	0:30:50	1:05:03	2:10:06
0:00:38	0:01:15	0:02:30	0:03:45	0:05:00	0:15:38	0:31:15	1:05:56	2:11:52
0:00:38	0:01:16	0:02:32	0:03:48	0:05:04	0:15:50	0:31:40	1:06:48	2:13:37
0:00:39	0:01:17	0:02:34	0:03:51	0:05:08	0:16:03	0:32:05	1:07:41	2:15:23
0:00:39	0:01:18	0:02:36	0:03:54	0:05:12	0:16:15	0:32:30	1:08:34	2:17:08
0:00:40	0:01:19	0:02:38	0:03:57	0:05:16	0:16:28	0:32:55	1:09:27	2:18:54

200m	400m	800m	1200m	1600m	5K	10K	13.1 mi.	26.2 mi.
0:00:40	0:01:20	0:02:40	0:04:00	0:05:20	0:16:40	0:33:20	1:10:19	2:20:39
0:00:41	0:01:21	0:02:42	0:04:03	0:05:24	0:16:53	0:33:45	1:11:12	2:22:24
0:00:41	0:01:22	0:02:44	0:04:06	0:05:28	0:17:05	0:34:10	1:12:05	2:24:10
0:00:42	0:01:23	0:02:46	0:04:09	0:05:32	0:17:18	0:34:35	1:12:58	2:25:55
0:00:42	0:01:24	0:02:48	0:04:12	0:05:36	0:17:30	0:35:00	1:13:50	2:27:41
0:00:43	0:01:25	0:02:50	0:04:15	0:05:40	0:17:43	0:35:25	1:14:43	2:29:26
0:00:43	0:01:26	0:02:52	0:04:18	0:05:44	0:17:55	0:35:50	1:15:36	2:31:12
0:00:44	0:01:27	0:02:54	0:04:21	0:05:48	0:18:08	0:36:15	1:16:29	2:32:57
0:00:44	0:01:28	0:02:56	0:04:24	0:05:52	0:18:20	0:36:40	1:17:21	2:34:43
0:00:45	0:01:29	0:02:58	0:04:27	0:05:56	0:18:33	0:37:05	1:18:14	2:36:28
0:00:45	0:01:30	0:03:00	0:04:30	0:06:00	0:18:45	0:37:30	1:19:07	2:38:14
0:00:46	0:01:31	0:03:02	0:04:33	0:06:04	0:18:58	0:37:55	1:20:00	2:39:59
0:00:46	0:01:32	0:03:04	0:04:36	0:06:08	0:19:10	0:38:20	1:20:52	2:41:45
0:00:47	0:01:33	0:03:06	0:04:39	0:06:12	0:19:23	0:38:45	1:21:45	2:43:30
0:00:47	0:01:34	0:03:08	0:04:42	0:06:16	0:19:35	0:39:10	1:22:38	2:45:16
0:00:48	0:01:35	0:03:10	0:04:45	0:06:20	0:19:48	0:39:35	1:23:31	2:47:01
0:00:48	0:01:36	0:03:12	0:04:48	0:06:24	0:20:00	0:40:00	1:24:23	2:48:47
0:00:49	0:01:37	0:03:14	0:04:51	0:06:28	0:20:13	0:40:25	1:25:16	2:50:32
0:00:49	0:01:38	0:03:16	0:04:54	0:06:32	0:20:25	0:40:50	1:26:09	2:52:18
0:00:50	0:01:39	0:03:18	0:04:57	0:06:36	0:20:38	0:41:15	1:27:02	2:54:03
0:00:50	0:01:40	0:03:20	0:05:00	0:06:40	0:20:50	0:41:40	1:27:54	2:55:49
0:00:51	0:01:41	0:03:22	0:05:03	0:06:44	0:21:03	0:42:05	1:28:47	2:57:34
0:00:51	0:01:42	0:03:24	0:05:06	0:06:48	0:21:15	0:42:30	1:29:40	2:59:20

⋯⟩

PACE CHART (continued)

200m	400m	800m	1200m	1600m	5K	10K	13.1 mi.	26.2 mi.
0:00:52	0:01:43	0:03:26	0:05:09	0:06:52	0:21:28	0:42:55	1:30:32	3:01:05
0:00:52	0:01:44	0:03:28	0:05:12	0:06:56	0:21:40	0:43:20	1:31:25	3:02:51
0:00:53	0:01:45	0:03:30	0:05:15	0:07:00	0:21:53	0:43:45	1:32:18	3:04:36
0:00:53	0:01:46	0:03:32	0:05:18	0:07:04	0:22:05	0:44:10	1:33:11	3:06:22
0:00:54	0:01:47	0:03:34	0:05:21	0:07:08	0:22:18	0:44:35	1:34:03	3:08:07
0:00:54	0:01:48	0:03:36	0:05:24	0:07:12	0:22:30	0:45:00	1:34:56	3:09:53
0:00:55	0:01:49	0:03:38	0:05:27	0:07:16	0:22:43	0:45:25	1:35:49	3:11:38
0:00:55	0:01:50	0:03:40	0:05:30	0:07:20	0:22:55	0:45:50	1:36:42	3:13:24
0:00:56	0:01:51	0:03:42	0:05:33	0:07:24	0:23:08	0:46:15	1:37:34	3:15:09
0:00:56	0:01:52	0:03:44	0:05:36	0:07:28	0:23:20	0:46:40	1:38:27	3:16:55
0:00:57	0:01:53	0:03:46	0:05:39	0:07:32	0:23:33	0:47:05	1:39:20	3:18:40
0:00:57	0:01:54	0:03:48	0:05:42	0:07:36	0:23:45	0:47:30	1:40:13	3:20:26
0:00:58	0:01:55	0:03:50	0:05:45	0:07:40	0:23:58	0:47:55	1:41:05	3:22:11
0:00:58	0:01:56	0:03:52	0:05:48	0:07:44	0:24:10	0:48:20	1:41:58	3:23:57
0:00:59	0:01:57	0:03:54	0:05:51	0:07:48	0:24:23	0:48:45	1:42:51	3:25:42
0:00:59	0:01:58	0:03:56	0:05:54	0:07:52	0:24:35	0:49:10	1:43:44	3:27:28
0:01:00	0:01:59	0:03:58	0:05:57	0:07:56	0:24:48	0:49:35	1:44:36	3:29:13
0:01:00	0:02:00	0:04:00	0:06:00	0:08:00	0:25:00	0:50:00	1:45:29	3:30:59
0:01:01	0:02:01	0:04:02	0:06:03	0:08:04	0:25:13	0:50:25	1:46:22	3:32:44
0:01:01	0:02:02	0:04:04	0:06:06	0:08:08	0:25:25	0:50:50	1:47:15	3:34:29
0:01:02	0:02:03	0:04:06	0:06:09	0:08:12	0:25:38	0:51:15	1:48:07	3:36:15
0:01:02	0:02:04	0:04:08	0:06:12	0:08:16	0:25:50	0:51:40	1:49:00	3:38:00
0:01:03	0:02:05	0:04:10	0:06:15	0:08:20	0:26:03	0:52:05	1:49:53	3:39:46

·····⟫

200m	400m	800m	1200m	1600m	5K	10K	13.1 mi.	26.2 mi.
0:01:03	0:02:06	0:04:12	0:06:18	0:08:24	0:26:15	0:52:30	1:50:46	3:41:31
0:01:04	0:02:07	0:04:14	0:06:21	0:08:28	0:26:28	0:52:55	1:51:38	3:43:17
0:01:04	0:02:08	0:04:16	0:06:24	0:08:32	0:26:40	0:53:20	1:52:31	3:45:02
0:01:05	0:02:09	0:04:18	0:06:27	0:08:36	0:26:53	0:53:45	1:53:24	3:46:48
0:01:05	0:02:10	0:04:20	0:06:30	0:08:40	0:27:05	0:54:10	1:54:17	3:48:33
0:01:06	0:02:11	0:04:22	0:06:33	0:08:44	0:27:18	0:54:35	1:55:09	3:50:19
0:01:06	0:02:12	0:04:24	0:06:36	0:08:48	0:27:30	0:55:00	1:56:02	3:52:04
0:01:07	0:02:13	0:04:26	0:06:39	0:08:52	0:27:43	0:55:25	1:56:55	3:53:50
0:01:07	0:02:14	0:04:28	0:06:42	0:08:56	0:27:55	0:55:50	1:57:47	3:55:35
0:01:08	0:02:15	0:04:30	0:06:45	0:09:00	0:28:08	0:56:15	1:58:40	3:57:21
0:01:08	0:02:16	0:04:32	0:06:48	0:09:04	0:28:20	0:56:40	1:59:33	3:59:06
0:01:09	0:02:17	0:04:34	0:06:51	0:09:08	0:28:33	0:57:05	2:00:26	4:00:52
0:01:11	0:02:22	0:04:44	0:07:06	0:09:28	0:29:35	0:59:10	2:04:49	4:09:39
0:01:14	0:02:28	0:04:56	0:07:24	0:09:52	0:30:50	1:01:40	2:10:06	4:20:12
0:01:17	0:02:33	0:05:06	0:07:39	0:10:12	0:31:53	1:03:45	2:14:30	4:29:00
0:01:21	0:02:42	0:05:24	0:08:06	0:10:48	0:33:45	1:07:30	2:22:24	4:44:49
0:01:26	0:02:51	0:05:42	0:08:33	0:11:24	0:35:38	1:11:15	2:30:19	5:00:38
0:01:30	0:02:59	0:05:58	0:08:57	0:11:56	0:37:18	1:14:35	2:37:21	5:14:42
0:01:34	0:03:07	0:06:14	0:09:21	0:12:28	0:38:58	1:17:55	2:44:23	5:28:46
0:01:38	0:03:16	0:06:32	0:09:48	0:13:04	0:40:50	1:21:40	2:52:18	5:44:36
0:01:43	0:03:25	0:06:50	0:10:15	0:13:40	0:42:43	1:25:25	3:00:12	6:00:25

OUR FAVES

Books

Anatomy for Runners: Unlocking Your Athletic Potential for Health, Speed, and Injury Prevention by Jay Dicharry

The Chimp Paradox: The Mind Management Program to Help You Achieve Success, Confidence, and Happiness by Steve Peters

The Desire Map: A Guide to Creating Goals with Soul by Danielle LaPorte

Paula: My Life so Far by Paula Radcliffe

Quiet: The Power of Introverts in a World that Can't Stop Talking by Susan Cain

Run to Overcome: The Inspiring Story of an American Champion's Long-Distance Quest to Achieve a Big Dream by Meb Keflezeghi

Spark: The Revolutionary New Science of Exercise and the Brain by John J. Ratey and Eric Hagerman

The Sports Gene: Inside the Science of Extraordinary Athletic Performance by David Epstein

Top Dog: The Science of Winning by Po Bronson and Ashley Merryman

Turning Pro: Tap Your Inner Power and Create Your Life's Work by Steven Pressfield

The War of Art: Break Through the Blocks and Win Your Inner Creative Battles by Steven Pressfield

Web Sites & Blogs

AskLaurenFleshman.com is a combination of storytelling and Q&A.

BelieveIAm.com is a collection of transformative designs and tools that share sports psychology techniques used by pro athletes—a relaxation mp3, race visualization, goal setting worksheets, race planning template, and more—that help women succeed in life and in sport by developing positive beliefs about themselves.

Dyestat.com, **Milesplit.com**, and **Runnerspace.com** are comprehensive sites with a high-school focus.

Flotrack.org is a running news site best known for its race coverage and athlete interviews.

Letsrun.com's homepage can't be beat for up-to-the-minute running news.

Oiselle is a women's running apparel company with a strong voice that shines a spotlight on sister heroes all over the world through social media and their award-winning blog. More info at oiselle.com or @oiselle on Twitter.

Nutrition

Picky Bars is a real-food performance bar company that Lauren and her husband, Jesse, founded in 2010 with pro marathoner Stephanie Rothstein Bruce. Picky Bars can be found at REI and lots of specialty stores. Join the Picky Club and get bars of your choosing delivered to your doorstep!

Group Runs

The Flock is Lauren's primary running community. This dues-based team is open to any woman who wants to race.

Use **localeikki** to find and share great places to run, walk, hike, and bike while on the road to make your health and travel planning easier.

Run with Ro is a weekly running group in Ro's hometown of Providence, RI. Organized by LadyProject.org, it's open to all runners. Enjoy the free 5K on the Boulevard in the summer months.

Music

Some people like hard-core rap blasting in their ears before competition; others like up-tempo techno; others like chilled-out beats. We've compiled our favorite inspirational tunes that amp us and help us BELIEVE a little more. Find our "BelieveJournal" playlist on **Spotify!**

Shoutouts!

Lauren: To my family who raised me, the family I married into, and most of all Jesse and Jude: thank you! The following also inspired these pages: Coaches DeLong, Evans, Lananna, Mahon, and Rowland. The Oiselle Nest. Sally Bergesen, Bob and Sarah Lesko, Little Wing. The Picky Crew. Ray Flynn, Shanna Burnette, John Ball, Jay Dicharry, Justine Lucia, Robyn Pester, Lance Deal, SMI, Rebound, Malindi Elmore, Nicole Teter, and my friends and teammates past and present.

Ro: A special thanks to Myles, Hope, and Ava; my parents and brother; Renee Jardine; Molly Huddle; Rose and Ben Keefe; Joanna Murphy; Noreen O'Reilly; Dr. Samantha O'Connell, and Ray Treacy. Also to my sisters in sport—Kim Smith, Mary Cullen, Stephanie Reilly, Amy Rudolph, Sarah Jamieson, Emer O'Shea, Meggie Smith, Morgan Sjörgen, Ann Gaffigan, Marie Davenport, and many more.

BELIEVE

Running serves as the perfect metaphor for life—that's the beauty of it all. The lessons you learn through setting and working toward goals can be applied in all other aspects of your life.

Relinquish the outcome

You have the right to work, but not to the fruits of the work. The success gods and good luck show up more often when the training and preparation has been done. But whatever happens—win or lose—just keep on running!

Take the risk

Accept that sport is inherently risky—the whole spectrum of human emotion, effort, and physicality is on display. You don't get to know the result in advance. But you get to play. You get to compete. You get to fight. You get to challenge. You get to work. You get to enjoy yourself. You get to be humbled. You get to feel fully alive in the moment. We must risk the agony of losing in the chance of experiencing the ecstasy of winning.

You are not what you do

Whether it's your 5K time or your job or your weight or your income, it does not determine your self-worth. True self-esteem is a reflection of living with integrity and pursuing meaningful goals. Let the benefits of being engaged and committed to your passion increase your self-esteem, deepen your joy, and raise the quality of your life!

Know that trying entails effort and patience

Embrace your gifts and put them to work. You've got to sow the seeds and tend to them: Pull the weeds, water the buds, and give it time. You can't force a flower to bloom. But in the right environment, with the right conditions, when the right season comes, the seeds will flourish.

Better me → better community → better world

Pursuing your running goals sometimes might feel like a selfish endeavor. But if running enhances your physical, mental and spiritual health, then collectively it enhances our community. And on a global scale, the running community is an amazing bunch. For example, the London Marathon holds the record for being the largest annual fundraiser in the world (e.g., raised over 49 million pounds in 2009), and that's just one race. Running adds so much value to so many people individually and collectively across the globe.

Be the best athlete you can be

While we can't guarantee that you'll win your next 5K, we hope we have helped you improve. Take action on the knowledge you've gathered. Keep learning. Keep the spokes of the wheel in check. Embrace your opportunity to experience the highs and lows of your running journey.

Do the training. Be open. Be aware. Be patient. Believe that your preparation will meet its opportunity, and that's when the magic will happen.

Lauren & Ro

BELIEVE IN YOU